STORIES OF COURAGE
AND INSPIRATION

FACING ADVERSITY

DR. JEFFREY L. GURIAN

Happiness Center Publications
New York, New York

HAPPINESS
CENTER
PUBLICATIONS

Interior Design by FormattedBooks.com

ISBN: 978-1-7354426-3-1 (paperback)

ABOUT THE AUTHOR

People often refer to Jeffrey Gurian as a "Renaissance Man" because he's involved in so many things. He's a former Cosmetic Dentist, and Clinical Prof. in Oral Medicine and Oro-Facial Pain at New York University, and a 20-year Board member  of The Association for Spirituality and Psychotherapy, besides being a comedy writer, performer, director, author, producer, and radio personality, ... and not always in that order.

But it wasn't exactly easy for him to accomplish all those things. He's had to battle fear all along the way, and overcome many obstacles and much adversity. Possibly inherited, or maybe internalized from an over-protective childhood, he never felt that the world was a safe place.

In his earlier book, "Healing Your Heart, By Changing Your Mind—A Spiritual and Humorous Approach To Achieving Happiness" which hit Best Seller status on Amazon, he explained how we all develop what he refers to as "heart wounds."

Starting from the time we're children, any time someone says something to hurt your feelings, or breaks a promise to you, lies to you, breaks up with you in a relationship, or hurts you in any way, we carry that energy inside of us in our heart chakras.

Basically we internalize what he calls "heart wounds" from unkind things that people have said to us, or from feelings of aloneness and "not being enough" that we develop for many possible reasons.

It could be caused by bullying, by discord in the home as a child, or sometimes it can even be from having learning disabilities that give us the idea that we're not as smart as other people, just because we process information in a different way.

This leads us into carrying negative messages about ourselves, which often translates into a negative worldview, confusion, and fear.

Jeffrey's own battles with what were diagnosed in later years as learning disabilities and a severe stutter, which started at age 6 or 7 and stayed with

Jeffrey@JeffreyGurian.com

him throughout his 20's and beyond, gave him the impetus to stand up to his fears.

Through many years of hard work, he was able to develop a cure for his stuttering, and presently as an avocation he works with stutterers from all over the world, to teach them how not to stutter.

He's learned to confront his fears on a daily basis, still not completely understanding the cause of them, but understanding that they would be very happy if he never accomplished anything and just stayed at home, in bed, under the covers where it always feels safe.

As a Board member of The Association for Spirituality and Psychotherapy since 1999, he's come to learn that millions of people experience fear as well, and that it often keeps them from achieving their goals.

Fear is a bully that needs to be stood up to and confronted, so that like most bullies it just slinks away. That is the reason he wrote this book and the previous two in what he refers to as his Happiness Series. It's a continuation of his previous books that teach people to examine their thoughts, and to see which thoughts they're holding about themselves that are not valid.

It's not an easy thing to examine your thoughts objectively, because we tend to believe all our thoughts. The important fact to remember is that we created all of our thoughts, and those thoughts are not necessarily based on our experience, but on our INTERPRETATION of our experience, which can be two very different things.

It's the reason why two children can grow up in the same household, with the same parents and be nothing alike, like two completely different people. And if you asked them about their childhood, you might think they grew up in two different homes.

The other important fact to remember is that any thought you create, you can also un-create, which is how he cured himself of stuttering by convincing his sub-conscious mind that he no longer "needed" to stutter. There was really nothing wrong with him. He created a "false disability" for himself.

In his last book on FEAR and how to conquer it, we learn how to convince our sub-conscious minds that there's really nothing to be afraid of by incorporating both a cognitive and Spiritual approach, with the understanding that "Fear is the Opposite of Faith", and that if your faith is strong there is no room in your life for fear.

Certain fear is reasonable of course, like fear of skydiving or engaging in a sport where there is the chance of being hurt, but the fear we're talking about is the fear that tells you that you can't accomplish your goals, because of something about yourself that isn't really true.

That's why this book is so important to him because the people discussed in this book have overcome the kind of adversity that stops most people, but they drew on the inner strength they often didn't know they had, and went on to achieve their goals despite the tremendous adversity they faced.

The author is an expert in fighting against fear, and he challenges himself all the time with things like a solo two-week trip to Japan, just because traveling is so difficult for him, and brings up every fear he could imagine. This includes fear of being lost, which he encountered every single day in his trip to Japan, trying to navigate the Japanese subway system.

His success in fighting the fear has allowed him to work and perform in the comedy world with legends like Rodney Dangerfield, Joan Rivers, George Wallace, Phil Hartman, Richard Belzer, Gilbert Gottfried, Jerry Lewis, and Andrew "Dice" Clay, among many others.

And for those of you old enough to remember, he even worked with Mr. Television, Milton Berle who was Jeffrey's sponsor in the legendary Friars Club.

As one of the only doctors with a long-standing career in comedy, Jeffrey has performed at most of the big clubs in N.Y. and L.A. and was featured several times on Comedy Central's hit Kroll Show with Nick Kroll, John Mulaney, Amy Poehler, Seth Rogen, Laura Dern and Katy Perry.

He was actually the first to be pranked with Too Much Tuna in the viral "Too Much Tuna" sketch on Kroll Show. He was also a regular on-air personality on Sirius XM's Bennington Show, (formerly Ron and Fez), for two years, where besides being on air, he also brought on special guests/friends like Russell Peters, Trevor Noah, Colin Quinn, Artie Lange, Susie Essman, D.L. Hughley, and Lisa Lampanelli. As of 2021 he still makes personal appearances on the show.

Besides having performed comedy on all the major stages in NY and LA, he's also a comedy journalist and has been covering the comedy scene since 1999. From 2014-2019 he wrote a weekly column covering the comedy scene for the top comedy website The Interrobang called "Jumping

Around With Jeffrey Gurian", and has also written for MTV, National Lampoon, Weekly World News, The Weekly Humorist and many Friars Roasts.

His Comedy Matters TV You Tube channel has over 500 A-list celebrity interviews including Jimmy Fallon, Judd Apatow, Marc Maron, Bill Burr, Tracy Morgan, Chelsea Handler, Jim Carrey, Trevor Noah, Lisa Lampanelli, Susie Essman, Nick Kroll, Amy Schumer, Gilbert Gottfried, John Mulaney, Amy Poehler, and many, many more, with well over two million views.

He's produced shows starring Kevin Hart and Susie Essman, and according to Paul Provenza and Nick Kroll is known by everyone in comedy. Nick says on camera that "nobody has more access to people in comedy than Jeffrey Gurian."

He filmed several episodes of Real Housewives of New York, in which he created a sketch for Countess LuAnn and Princess Carole Radziwill. He also recently filmed an episode of Crashing at the request of director Judd Apatow.

Two of his greatest accomplishments discussed in detail in this book were surviving a "widow-maker" heart attack in 2015, and being hospitalized in March of 2020 for Covid 19 double pneumonia!

This is his 8ᵗʰ book. His 6ᵗʰ book, which hit Best Seller status on Amazon was the first of what he calls his "Happiness Series" and is called "Healing Your Heart, By Changing Your Mind—A Spiritual and Humorous Approach To Achieving Happiness" It has over 250 mostly five-star reviews, and is available as an e-book, a paperback and an audio book. This is the link to the book:
https://www.amazon.com/dp/0692982515

His last book, the 2ⁿᵈ in his Happiness Series is called "Fight The Fear-Overcoming Obstacles That Stand In Your Way" and opened as a #1 Release on Amazon in several categories including Medicine and Psychology, Group Therapy, Attention Deficit Disorder, and Adult Children of Alcoholics.

It has over 80 mostly five-star reviews and is available as an e-book and a paperback. This is the link to that book:
https://www.amazon.com/dp/1735442607

Jeffrey hopes you enjoy this 3ʳᵈ book in the Happiness Series and go on to "Fight the Fear" and overcome adversity in your own lives!

To sign up for Jeffrey's mailing list and receive a free gift, and/or if you need coaching, a complimentary 15 minute private Skype call with

Jeffrey, please enter your e-mail on the landing page on his website at
https://mailchi.mp/jeffreygurian/healingyourheart

For more on Jeffrey visit his website at
https://www.comedymatterstv.com

For help with stuttering go to:
https://www.stopstutteringnowgurian.com

And please subscribe to his Comedy Matters TV channel on You Tube at
https://www.youtube.com/comedymatterstv

To support his work go to:
https://www.patreon.com/comedymatterstv

On IG he's @JeffreyGurian

Jeffrey would LOVE to hear from you!

PREFACE

"Obstacles" in life can come in many forms. They can be caused by illness, accidents, birth defects, and bad choices. This book is a compilation of public stories about people who have faced seemingly insurmountable types of adversities and somehow managed to rise above them.

I have been collecting stories like these for the last twenty plus years because the courage of these people fascinates me. This book is for anyone who feels that life has dealt them a difficult hand. Hopefully these stories will inspire you to keep on going no matter what.

Life is hard for everyone. Of that there is no doubt. For some of us though it's harder than for others. Being born itself is a miracle, understanding that those two particular cells joined, kept splitting, and wound up becoming YOU!

And if you came out alright, which means that all of the cells had to know exactly where to go and how to create all the right parts that function properly, that is even more of a miracle.

But every once in a while there's an error of some kind. Something goes wrong leading to some kind of illness or syndrome, or defect and as that person develops from an infant into adulthood, they have to find ways to cope with what some might consider to be an "obstacle."

However, what some might consider to be an "obstacle" others look at as a challenge. Those are the people I want to honor in this book.

It's always been fascinating to me, how some people crumble from the hand they were given, and others find the strength to rise above it. This is not being judgmental by any means. Not everyone has it in them to rise above their "obstacle" but enough do to give others hope that they too can do the same.

As you persevere and ultimately succeed you become an inspiration to others.

Somehow, I've always been drawn to these stories, and twenty-one years ago, in the year 1999 I began collecting them from newspapers and magazines until I wound up with a folder bursting with those kinds of stories. I find them to be incredibly inspirational, which led me to want to do this book.

In my own life I feel like I have fought against many obstacles to try and overcome them, the most dramatic possibly being my stuttering problem that started around age 6 or 7 and lasted well into my 20's and beyond.

I've also had to deal with real life problems like severe learning disabilities, a sleep disorder that makes studying very difficult, serious illness in the form of a "widowmaker" heart attack, Covid Double Pneumonia, depression, divorce, hospitalization, and negativity from people who should have known better, and who told me that I would never be successful and tried to stand in the way of my success.

After many, many years of hard work I managed to completely cure myself of stuttering and now as an avocation I work with stutterers all over the world, to teach them how NOT to stutter.

I was lucky enough to survive both of those serious health problems I experienced, got through the divorce and today have a very friendly relationship with my ex, where I go to her house and celebrate holidays with her and her husband, and all of our children combined. I have a big extended family thanks to leading my life according to certain principles. Ancient Spiritual principles! And they are very powerful!

In the time it took for me to recover from Covid Double Pneumonia when I was literally afraid to leave the house, I decided to use that time to write this book which I had been wanting to write for many years, turning a negative into a positive.

I sought help for depression and learned to fight it without medication, because unfortunately no medication has ever worked for me. I fought it by incorporating those same Spiritual principles into my life so that I could think differently, and found the inner strength to stand up to the bullies, and the people who tried to convince me that I'd never be successful.

Every single one of us has something about ourselves that we would change if we could. The Serenity Prayer says it best, "Grant me the Serenity to accept the things I cannot change, the courage to change the things I can, and the Wisdom to know the difference."

The last line is the most important. The "Wisdom" to know the difference. If I was not given the Grace to understand that I could cure myself of stuttering, and that for whatever reason I had created it with my own mind, I would still be stuttering today.

It was a false disability I had created with my six or seven-year-old mind that is not valid for me today as an adult. If I had an important decision to make in my life, I would never ask a six or seven-year-old what they thought I should do. But here I was an adult thinking I needed to stutter because a 6 or 7-year-old "me" thought it would be a good idea!

You'll notice I take the liberty of capitalizing certain words I think carry great importance. If you're an English teacher, don't worry, ... you'll get used to it.

This book is dedicated to all those people who had the courage to either change or if they had something they couldn't change, who had the courage and inner strength to rise above it. I salute them!

All the stories in this book have already been made public, so I'm not exposing anyone. I am honoring their accomplishments by including them in this compilation of my personal heroes.

Rather than separating them into the type of obstacles people face, I decided to separate them by the years during which I found them. Some years have many stories, and some have very few.

There are even some years that are not represented at all, and I couldn't begin to tell you why. I guess no stories caught my eye in those years, but each and every one that I do have is very special. Of course, there are literally thousands more I don't know about. These are only the ones that crossed my path.

So the next time you're in the space of feeling sorry for yourself, hopefully you'll read this book and give yourself the power to carry on. Remember, self-pity is one of the worst things you can do to yourself, and fear is a bully that tells you you'll never succeed or get the things you want, but it's more important to remember that no obstacle can stand in your way!

DEDICATION

I'd like to dedicate this book to my parents Marjorie and Raymond Gurian who had great faith in me and told me there was nothing I couldn't accomplish, to my sister Ronnie who has overcome many obstacles of her own, and to my two amazing daughters Elizabeth and Kathryn who gave me the two greatest gifts any man could have, the gift of being a father and grandfather.

TABLE OF CONTENTS

CHAPTER 1

From The Year 1999

Top Model Born With No Legs

On May 25th 1999, an article appeared in the New York Post about model Aimee Mullins. At the time Aimee was 23, had just been photographed for the Anne Klein "Significant Women" campaign, and had recently been featured in People Magazine's "50 Most Beautiful People In The World."

What made her different than the other models on the catwalk was that she was a double amputee. Born with no fibulas, doctors told her parents that if she didn't have her lower legs amputated, she'd spend the rest of her life in a wheelchair.

At one year old she had her first surgery, followed by several others in later years. She got prosthetic legs and is quoted as saying that she never uses her prosthetic legs as an excuse for anything. She said, "I don't consider myself disabled at all."

She also said "If you want to get technical about it, I'm a bilateral below-the-knee amputee. But that's a feature of my body. It's not me."

In 1996 she entered the Paralympics and set a world record for the 200-meter run which she did in 34.06 seconds. She said she sees her legs as "working pieces of art."

That Paralympic win led her to be asked by designer Alexander McQueen to model in his spring 1999 show wearing McQueen-designed prosthetic limbs. They were legs ending in 6-inch stylish boots.

She refused to do any interviews that would turn her into a human-interest story. Her words, "Don't turn me into a tragic heroine. There's nothing tragic about it."

In 2009 she did a TED talk about her now 12 pairs of legs which she has custom made in the south of England.

Height Was No Obstacle To Them

It was 1999 when Amy Roloff was profiled in Mc-Call's magazine, and the following year her husband Matt Roloff was profiled in People Magazine.

They were both 4'2" and born with different types of dwarfism. Matt's type of dwarfism, which causes bone and joint deformities left him with the need to use crutches after enduring more than ten surgeries over a period of three years as a child, to try and correct his twisted legs.

He spent several months in a body cast and endured excruciating pain. As an adult he did some film work playing an Ewok in the film "Return of the Jedi" and went on to become a high-end computer software salesman.

In 1989 while on a business trip to Oregon he happened to find a run-down farmhouse in a town called Hillsdale and bought it for $185,000. Then he proceeded to build his dream house including a replica of an Old West town in his backyard.

It's a 35-acre playland for he and his four kids, including a set of twins, only one of whom inherited dwarfism. He himself was an inch too short to ever go on any rides at amusement parks, so he built his own.

It took four years to build but besides the Old West town, his home features a huge tree house, a 70-foot-long mine shaft, a soccer field and 300 feet of underground tunnels. A child's delight. Neighbor's children were always welcome to come and play.

Amy was convinced that she'd never be married or have children, but in 1986 she gave in and attended a Little People of America's conference in Dearborn, Michigan where she met Matt, who at the time was living in San Jose, California.

They corresponded for six months when Matt invited her to come and visit him in San Jose. She had never done anything like that before, but she went and had the time of her life. The following year they were married, and wound up having four children. They stayed married for 27 years until their divorce in 2015.

In 2005 they began starring in the TLC reality show Little People, Big World which lasted for six seasons, and then starting in 2012 they started doing specials for TLC which also ran in 2013.

Matt also has a number of other businesses as a motivational speaker, and running Direct Access Solutions, a company that provides accessibility products for little people in the hospitality industry. He's also the author of three books, was the President of Little People of America, and is an activist for short-statured people.

He's even traveled to Iraq three times to visit U.S. troops and help an Iraqi family get medical attention for their three children with dwarfism.

Both Matt and Amy went on to have new love relationships proving that size doesn't really matter.

Leprechauns And Ewoks

It must be difficult to lead your life as a little person, but many little people have been determined to lead meaningful lives, as is the case with Warwick Davis, who was written about in the NY Post back in 1999.

He's from Great Britain and stands just 3' 6" tall, but his size specifically enabled him to play a murderous Irish fairy in a gory horror series called "Leprechaun."

It also brought controversy as certain Irish groups were offended by what they took as an insult to their culture.

At only 11 years of age, and just 2' 11" tall, after being encouraged by his grandmother, Warwick landed the role of the Ewok creature Cricket, in the Star Wars classic "Return of the Jedi" and became one of the series most popular minor characters.

At the time of the writing of the article he was reprising his role as Wicket in a film called "Episode 1: The Phantom Menace."

When he played his first evil role in "Leprechaun" he wound up working with co-star Jennifer Aniston. He said, "It is every actor's dream to play an evil character, a part to really get your thespian teeth into."

The part required him to go through three hours of make-up every day for a month. He wound up doing three sequels over the next six years, which led him to open his own talent agency called Willow Management for actors under 5 feet tall.

He jokingly said, "People start off in fairly small parts, if you'll pardon the pun."

The 5'4' Basketball Star

It seemed that 1999 seemed to be the year for stories on height, and Shawnta Rogers made for a great story in the NY Post. At 5' 4" you wouldn't expect him to be a basketball star, but those who saw him play at Washington State University thought he could possibly be the best point guard in the nation.

The writer opened the story by saying, "There comes a time in a man's life when he must hear about his shortcomings—unsolicited of course. The words feel like a howitzer, shredding skin, bone and finally soul, until the self-portrait is smashed into a billion pieces."

He went on to say, "The ego eventually regenerates because the moment always passes—thankfully."

But what if the moment doesn't pass? What if people continuously remind you of your shortcomings? Not only people you know but strangers who feel they have the right to make comments about you, or your appearance.

In Shawnta's case during games other students would yell out the Smurf theme song, probably patting themselves on the back for being so clever, instead of paying respect to a man who was able to stand up to players who were 6'9", a whole foot and a half taller than him.

They also called him Tattoo in reference to Herve Villechaise, the little person who starred in the TV show "Fantasy Island" and wound up committing suicide. Then they would alternate between calling him midget, dwarf, shrimp, and shorty, … this from all the "big men" who took credit for their genetics.

Many men think you have to "bust balls" in order to be considered a man. I reject that notion. Kids seem to have a mean streak where they pick a kid they think doesn't fit in and make his or her life miserable. But making fun of people is supposed to stop when you're about 10 years old. Several of our school shootings have been attributed to kids who had been bullied.

Adults are not supposed to be making fun of people. It's a form of bullying. And if you call them on it, the usual response is, "Hey, I was just kidding. It's just a joke!" And my response would be, "Oh yeh, well I have a pretty good sense of humor, explain the joke to me because I didn't get it."

Which would usually be followed by some kind of statement like, "You're too sensitive." Well, the truth is I'm exactly as sensitive as I'm supposed to be. You're just a jerk, and there are so many things I could make fun of about YOU, but I wouldn't stoop to doing that."

If that sounds personal, it is because I skipped a couple of grades as a kid, and being two years younger than all the other kids in my grade, I was always much smaller, but as I grew up, I learned to never allow "jokes" made at my expense. And in the world of comedy where I spend a lot of time, that kind of thing is very common, but not with me.

No one does that with me because they can tell I don't stand for it. It's not that I'm too sensitive, it's that I have respect for myself.

Rather than laugh politely, as many people do to show that they don't care, I wouldn't laugh at all. In one of my earlier books, the Amazon best seller "Healing Your Heart, By Changing Your Mind— A Spiritual and Humorous Approach To Achieving Happiness" I named these little "jokes" heart wounds.

We start accumulating them as children. We get one every time someone hurts your feelings, says something or does something to hurt you, breaks a promise to you, or breaks up with you in a relationship.

That stupid saying you learn as a child, "Sticks and stones will break your bones, but words can never harm you" is so far from the truth, because all of the bruises you got as a child healed up a long time ago, but each one of us can recall something that someone said that hurt our feelings as if it was yesterday, even if it was decades ago.

And these heart wounds stay with you for your entire life. They affect your self-esteem and your self-confidence, and every single decision you make in your life.

Every time you are called upon to make a decision, you think about what you should do. You use your thoughts to figure it out. And if some of your thoughts are faulty and negative about yourself, your decisions are not going to work out very well. They will be based on incorrect thoughts.

So you wind up getting the same job over and over again that doesn't work out, or you wind up in the same relationship that always seems to end badly, and the only common denominator in all of those things is you. You are the one who keeps showing up!

An important thought to have is that "you can't get better with the same mind that got you sick in the first place." You already know all of your own thoughts, and if those thoughts are not working for you, you need new thoughts.

The important fact to know is that you created all your thoughts, and any thought you created you can also uncreate. It takes a lot of hard work, but you can do it.

But first you have to identify the thoughts that are not valid for you. I've been doing it all my life, and it is one of the ways I cured myself of a severe stutter. I had to release the negative thoughts about myself that led to me feeling the "need" to stutter.

Examining your own thoughts is not an easy process because we tend to believe our thoughts. But the important fact here again is to realize that we created all of our thoughts, and our thoughts are not necessarily based on our experience, but instead they're based on our INTERPRETATION of our experience.

It's the reason that siblings who grew up in the same household with the same parents could describe their childhoods very differently, because of the way they interpreted their experiences. So, it's important to realize that many of the thoughts we use on a daily basis may not be valid for us.

But back to Shawnta, ... during the Atlantic 10 Conference tournament, which I'm guessing is very important, he was taunted by the entire opposing team, saying things like "Stand up Shawnta, ... we can't see you!"

And Shawnta didn't let it bother him. He sank a three-point shot to win the game, and had scored 28 points, seven assists, four rebounds, and four steals. According to his coach he dominated the game and was named the Atlantic 10 player of the year.

After high school he went on to play pro ball both in the United States and on several European teams. Go Shawnta!!!

Not Only Men Get Teased And Bullied

In 1999 when this article came out in People Magazine, Cheryl Haworth was a 16-year-old girl who was 5'9" and weighed 290 pounds. She was also able to clean-and-jerk 290 pounds, which she did on live television with Regis and Cathie Lee, a popular show in the United States.

She had to endure a lot of teasing growing up, and had started lifting weights at 12 years old to strengthen herself to play softball. At 16 years old she was already a gold medal favorite at the 2000 Sydney Olympic Games, where women's weightlifting made its Olympic debut.

Even at her size and weight she was flexible enough to do splits and a 30-inch vertical jump. She's the only school age child to ever hold adult U.S. records.

She said it gave her a lift to find out that her weight could be a plus in something. She was quoted as saying, "Even though I'm walking around school and I'm way heavier than everybody, I just think to myself, I'm in better shape than you are. It just doesn't look like it!"

Before she retired from the sport Cheryl went on to represent the United States in the Olympics, winning a bronze medal in 2000, a Champion Award at the Pan Am Games in 1999, a Champion Award at the Goodwill Games in 2001, and was inducted into the USA Weightlifting Hall of Fame in 2015.

In 2012, a documentary titled "Strong" was done about her efforts at the end of her career to compete in the 2008 Summer Olympics in Beijing.

Thalidomide Defects Couldn't Stop Him

During the late 1950's and early 60's many pregnant women all over the world were given the drug Thalidomide supposedly to help them with their morning sickness, not knowing that it created severe birth defects.

The babies, known as "Thalidomide babies," usually had hands that were attached to their shoulders, and severe deformities of their legs. The drug wasn't banned until 1961, and in Germany alone it was estimated that 10,000 babies were born with Thalidomide deformities.

On Nov. 9, 1959 Thomas Quasthoff was born in Hildesheim, Germany and was one of those babies. When he was less than a year old, he was in the children's ward of a hospital where nurses played recorded music to try and keep the children calm.

The following day, at less than one year old, Thomas was heard singing one of the melodies. His mother didn't believe it when the nurses told her because she said, "He's not able to speak, much less sing."

As an infant he spent a year and a half in a plaster cast to straighten his twisted legs. At 6 years old he was placed in an institution and his father had to fight for the right to take him home.

At the time of the writing of the People Magazine article I saw in 1999, Thomas had reached the age of 39 and was a star of the classical music

world, having put out 20 CD's, and having performed in concerts all over the world.

Standing at a little over 4 feet tall, he had earlier
been refused a place at a school for the performing
arts because they said it was impossible for him to
play the piano.

New York Philharmonic guest conductor Sir
Colin Davis is quoted as saying, "He is one of the
great bass-baritones of our time. To me he is a
lesson in life."

Because he was rejected from a top music
school his parents hired a voice coach with whom
he worked for 17 years. His big break finally came
in 1988 when he won Germany's prestigious ARD
International Music Competition leading to many
bookings and recording contracts.

A famous conductor heard him sing and invited
him to perform in the United States at a big event
in Eugene, Oregon. He's done several concerts here
in America and he says he likes it here because
"Americans respect accomplishment."

In line with the bullying comments I discussed
earlier, he was once called a "gnome" by a hate-
ful German critic. His response was, "I think it's
important to accept your disability. If you don't

love people, … and that includes yourself, … you shouldn't be in this business."

He's been the recipient of many awards and one of the best was in 2006 when he married a German TV journalist named Claudia Stelzig. That's so fantastic, yet the singles bars are filled with tall handsome guys with two legs, who can't get a date!

Thalidomide was banned for use in pregnancy in 1961, a bit too late, but is currently being used again as a cancer drug.

Losing A Leg, Gaining A Famous Husband

In 1999 Heather Mills was a 25-year-old model who had recently come back from helping war victims in Bosnia. In a freak accident she stepped off the curb not being able to see around a double-decker bus and was hit by a racing police motorcycle which tore off her left leg below the knee.

When she woke up in the hospital, she found that besides the loss of her leg, she had a punctured lung, and a fractured pelvis. The irony hit her that she had just returned from a war-torn area totally unharmed and then this happens in her own hometown.

In a classic example of turning a negative into a positive, a year later she founded the Heather Mills Health Trust to recycle artificial limbs to poor amputees all over the world.

Most prostheses need to be replaced as the remaining part of the limb heals. She realized this when she had to replace her first artificial leg after only five weeks and the hospital planned to discard it.

After a lot of hard work and lobbying she finally got hospitals to donate their used prostheses, and in 1994 she loaded up two trucks with 5,000 artificial limbs and 500 wheelchairs and brought them to Zagreb, Croatia. The U.N. estimated that more than 300,000 people had lost limbs in that area of the world, due to land mines and mortars.

Thanks to her and her charity more than 27,000 people had received recycled limbs at the time of the article. The Croatian ambassador to Great Britain said of her, "She managed with extraordinary resilience to turn her misfortune into a powerful vehicle for helping others."

Heather had a very rough childhood, with her mother leaving her family for another man when Heather was just 9, and then her father was imprisoned for fraud, leaving her and her sister to fend for themselves. For a time, she was homeless and briefly lived under a bridge.

After marrying at 17, and later becoming a model at 21, she eventually landed a million-dollar contract with an Italian cosmetics company. No one could have guessed that the year after the article I read was written she would meet Paul McCartney.

She and Paul were married in 2002, had a daughter and divorced in 2008. After her divorce she became very active in animal rights advocacy and is also the vice-president of the Limbless Association.

CHAPTER 2

From The Year 2000

From Homeless To Harvard

I remember reading this story when it first hit the newspapers and feeling tears well up in my eyes, and it was 20 years ago. Maybe because I have a daughter named Liz.

Liz Murray grew up in The Bronx, in a run-down apartment in a bad neighborhood, with two caring but drug addicted parents who mainlined drugs in front of her from the time she was a baby. They used their disability and welfare checks to buy heroin and cocaine.

At the time of the article I read, she was 19 years old. When she was 10 years old, her mother staggered in drunk one night and confessed to having AIDS. Liz didn't even know what that was at the time.

Three years later her Mom left to try and kick her drug habit, and went to live with a godfather, and Liz stayed with her Dad. But her Dad ran out of money and lost the apartment. He moved into a shelter and Liz was in the 8th grade for the second time. The school knew that something was wrong but didn't know what.

For a while Liz moved in with her mother, but the godfather she was living with didn't really want kids around, or even the sick woman anymore who by this time had developed full blown AIDS, and he made Liz's life very difficult.

At 15 she wound up alone on the street. When she turned 16 her mother died of AIDS and TB. She said it was then that she knew she had to turn her life around. She had been going to JFK high school which made the story even more powerful for me, because it was right down the block from my office at the time.

She realized she needed a job and got one at New York Public Interest Resource Group, an environmental, consumer–advocacy group, which she said helped her to develop great communication skills.

She solicited donations for the group going door to door, and managed to save a few thousand dollars over the summer.

She heard about an alternative high school called "Humanities Preparatory Academy" for special needs kids and she wanted to be accepted there so badly that she got her father out of the shelter and cleaned him up for an interview, using a friend's address as her own.

She was admitted the week before her 17th birthday and re-started high school, and she promised herself that she was going to work hard and graduate as soon as she could. She did the four years in two by working really hard, and doubling her course load by enrolling in early morning and weekend classes.

After winning a school trip to Boston she got the opportunity to walk through the Harvard campus and decided that's where she belonged. She was quoted as saying, "I couldn't believe that people were lucky enough to study in a place like this. My whole life had robbed me of opportunities like this. This is where I needed to be."

She graduated from the academy with almost a 100 average, but now she had to figure out how to get accepted at Harvard, and how to pay for it once she did. She found a scholarship for $12,000. a year being offered by the New York Times and the application consisted of an essay asking, "What obstacles have you overcome in your life to get where you are?" It was custom made for her.

She won the scholarship, but Harvard was hesitant about accepting someone with only two years of schooling, so she was waitlisted. But after they met her at her interview and heard her story, they opened up a spot for her.

She said when they handed her a course catalogue it was "something out of a fairy tale."

At the time of the article in 2000, she was lecturing to school children in between her classes, and volunteered for environmental and AIDS causes. Her father now had AIDS as well but was getting help and was in good spirits. She left Harvard in 2003 to take care of him and returned to Harvard in 2006. He eventually succumbed to AIDS. She graduated in 2009.

A made for TV movie about her life was done in 2003 called "Homeless to Harvard: The Liz Murray

Story" and in 2010 she released her New York Times bestselling memoir "Breaking Night." In 2018 she was profiled by Oprah on the OWN Network, and is married to her high school sweetheart James and has two beautiful children.

Female Gangbanger Marries Lawyer And Goes Straight

The year 2000 seemed to be the year for women and incredible life make-overs. Before she was 16 Isis Sapp-Grant was a founding member of a Brooklyn all girl street gang who beat people with baseball bats, and slashed people's faces just to see blood. She was angry all the time.

She took her gang to terrorize people in the subways, and had about 20 members under her rule. She said she didn't come from poverty and that her mother was very "cultural." She also said that "learning how to be a proper young woman wasn't the thing to do." She felt she excelled at "one-punch knockout."

Her robberies afforded her a street wardrobe and lots of gold chains and jewelry, and she said she kept a dark outfit handy because she would be going to at least one funeral a month.

What turned her around was one particular arrest where she found herself in handcuffs, and in her mind she likened it to the chains of her ancestors. She said she thought to herself, "Many people who came from Africa didn't have a choice about being in chains, and here I was doing it to myself."

It was like an epiphany. She sought help from her parents, her school, and even the police, and wound up going to college getting a bachelor's degree from SUNY/Stony Brook and then her Master's in social work from NYU.

At the time the article came out she was 29 and she had become a social worker using her experience to try and persuade girls not to join gangs. She started the Youth Empowerment Mission, was married to a corporate lawyer, had a son and lived in a brownstone in Brooklyn.

She Lived In Grand Central Terminal For Four Years

Another year 2000 miracle was the story of Tina S. The article I read didn't divulge her last name, but she spent four of her teenage years during the mid-80's living in Grand Central Station in New York City.

Living with her Mom and her Mom's drug dealer boyfriend in a welfare hotel was too much for her. She had been living with her Mom in a house in Astoria when the house burned down, and they were forced to move into the welfare hotel. But the fighting between her Mom and her Mom's boyfriend was just too much for her, so in 1985 she moved into Grand Central terminal with another homeless girl named April.

She lived mostly in a candle lit abandoned subway car with the seats ripped out, and the windows spray-painted black. She washed herself under a spigot in Grand Central or at the home of a regular subway rider named Max who let her come over once a week to take a shower and then gave her a few bucks and some food.

She'd sleep in boiler rooms, cardboard boxes or train tunnels, and when her friend April tried crack, she put if off for a while, but then succumbed to the temptation and tried it as well. That led to a three-year crack habit, during which she did whatever she could to get money.

That led to being raped in one of the tunnels, and an unrelated 8-month prison sentence. Eventually her friend April committed suicide by shooting herself in the head on the steps of a church, and Tina also thought about that as a way out of her situation.

She told herself, "Before I become an old bag lady, I would kill myself." But as she tells it, an "act of G-d" saved her in the form of a homeless advocate named George McDonald who worked around the area.

He convinced her to go to a two-year rehab program in upstate New York and helped her to get in. She was kicked out after a year for breaking the rules, but was already clean and sober and had managed to get her high school equivalency diploma.

She came back to the city and began working with an organization called Ready, Willing and Able which is an organization that teaches job skills to homeless people. She got on a house renovation crew.

At the time of this article I read in the NY Post, she was 31 years old, living in Brooklyn with a roommate, 2 dogs and a cat, and had just written a book about her experiences. It's called "Living At The Edge of the World—A Teenager's Survival In The Tunnels of Grand Central Station."

She said she didn't want people to feel sorry for her because as she said, "I could have been killed plenty of times. I'm lucky to be alive and not in some psychiatric ward."

As I do with each of these cases I write about, I tried to get current information about her but was not able to find any.

Asperger's Savants

In October of 2000, the New York Post did a story on Asperger's Syndrome, a rare but high-functioning form of autism that can exhibit many unusual traits.

About 10% of the autism community has what they refer to as "savant" abilities. They are abilities that most people would give anything to have. People with the syndrome show a wide range of intelligence and ability to comprehend things.

They may also have unusual speech patterns and impaired social skills, but often have other abilities that would qualify them as geniuses.

For instance, award-winning New York film-maker Lizzie Gottlieb made a documentary about her brother Nicky called "Today's Man". Nicky has

Asperger's Syndrome who according to his sister, as a toddler learned to speak Italian in two weeks, and by 4 or 5 years old would ask people their birthdates and the year they were born, and would immediately be able to tell them what day of the week that was.

Not long after he was born, he began having seizures and brain rhythms that often indicate what they called in those days "mental retardation", but what we now might refer to as developmental disabilities.

Doctors weren't sure whether he'd be able to walk and talk and he did both. It was during a childhood trip to Italy that doctors warned against taking, thinking that hearing another language would confuse him, that Nicky learned to speak Italian in just those few days.

In those days no one had a diagnosis for what he was exhibiting. They didn't think he was autistic, just very unusual. When he was 6, he had to watch the first half of "The Sound of Music" every single night and would scream if he couldn't see it. He was looking to put some order into his life by having a routine of some kind.

In the trailer I saw on the internet at his 21st birthday, which is where the documentary starts, he had the self-awareness to describe himself as being a man physically but mentally just a boy. I thought that was fascinating that he knew that and could verbalize it.

Examples of other so called "autistic savants" they mentioned were Richard Wawro who though autistic and legally blind started drawing at age 3 in chalk, by 6 had graduated to crayons and as an adult has sold more than 1,000 paintings, with people like Margaret Thatcher and Pope John Paul II as patrons.

Then there was Tony DeBlois of Massachusetts, who as an infant, born weighing only 1 pound and ¾ of an ounce, would scream if his mother turned off the radio. As a toddler he played rhythms on coffee cans, and by the age of 2 could actually imitate any melody on a tabletop organ and began playing the piano.

As an adult, although also blind as a result of being given too much oxygen at his premature birth, he went on to learn to play 20 instruments and has performed in concerts worldwide.

He was the subject of a TV movie called "Journey of the Heart" in 1997 with Cybill Shepherd and appeared himself at the end playing the piano.

Another amazing example of an autistic savant mentioned in the article was New Yorker George Finn who was profiled on the show "60 Minutes" and who has the ability to recall every single day of his life.

He can't add two plus two or five times seven, but he can identify the day of the week of any date you give him in history within seconds, and tell you what the weather was that day as well. This was confirmed by Morley Safer on the show "60 Minutes" which George jokingly said he'll remember for the rest of his life, and he wasn't kidding.

My last example is a man named Leslie Lemke born with glaucoma, cerebral palsy, and severe brain damage. To make matters worse they had to remove his eyes. Given up for adoption he was taken in by a kind family, the Lemkes.

For seven years he made no noises or showed any emotion and didn't learn to walk until he was 15.

But at 16 his adopted mother was awakened by hearing piano music and thought that her husband had left the TV on. She was astonished to find that with no musical training, Leslie was playing Tchaikovsky's "Piano Concerto No. 1" with absolute perfection after hearing it only one time. He played it on a little secondhand piano his mother had put in his bedroom to entertain him.

He also learned to sing along with his piano playing although he was not able to speak, and he has since performed several concerts in front of large audiences.

It seems that these people are able to use parts of their brain that most people cannot access. If we were able to access those parts of our brain, we might all have the ability to do these amazing things.

You might say that these people did not overcome their obstacles by using their will or their inner strength alone, and truthfully they probably had little to do with the fact of their special gifts, but I think they overcame their obstacles through Grace, and that the stories are powerful enough to belong in this book, because they are truly inspirational to anyone who has a child with autism, or any other so-called "disability."

Internationally Known Brain Surgeon Told He Was Not Fit For Med School

Also in the year 2000 I read an article about Dr. Fred Epstein an internationally known pediatric neurosurgeon who pioneered certain surgical techniques for the removal of tumors on the spinal cord and brainstem that before him were considered inoperable.

The reason he belongs in this book is because as a young boy he suffered with severe learning disabilities. He read slowly, had trouble making sense of numbers, and wrote the letter "e" backwards. He was told that he wasn't fit to go to medical school or to become a doctor.

So instead, he worked harder than all the other students, and graduated from New York University and New York Medical College. He did his internship and surgical residency at Montefiore Medical Center in the Bronx, and his neurosurgical residency at New York University–Bellevue Medical Center.

He did at least 3,000 neurosurgical operations for free on children whose parents couldn't afford his services. He became President of the International Society of Pediatric Neurosurgery, and published more than 175 scholarly papers besides being editor in chief of The Journal of Pediatric Neurosurgery.

Unfortunately, this brilliant man tragically passed away the next year in 2001 after falling off a bicycle, landing on his head, and splitting his helmet open ironically leading to severe brain damage. He was in a coma for 26 days and in the hospital for nine months before he succumbed.

I relate to his story a great deal, because when I was finally tested for my own learning disabilities as an adult, the doctor whose specialty it was to test for these things said he was amazed that I was ever able to get through dental school and graduate in the top half of my class because I exhibited such confusion. I had to learn that I process information in a different way than most people do.

He said that I probably had to work ten times as hard as everyone else which was true, but I was so determined to achieve my goal, there was no way I would ever give up.

Too Tall For Hollywood

Also in the year 2000, actress Allison Janney, who at six feet tall was always told she was too tall for Hollywood, never gave up and was cast as White

House Press Secretary C.J. Cregg in the NBC hit show The West Wing.

When not acting, and waiting patiently for her break, she had formerly supported herself by waitressing and scooping ice cream in New York City, proving that if you believe in yourself and persevere, you can make anything happen.

Too Short For Hollywood

In that very same year almost the exact reverse story happened when 3'10" Debbie Lee Carrington was cast to play "Mini-Mimi" on The Drew Carey Show. She was playing a mini version of Drew's nemesis Mimi Bobeck, played by Kathy Kinney.

Diagnosed with dwarfism at age 6 she didn't let it stop her from becoming a cheerleader in high school and winning 28 film roles by the year 2000, her first being cast as a "Munchkin" in 1981's film "Under the Rainbow."

She was also a stunt woman and appeared in many more films in years to come like "Men in Black", and "Return of the Jedi", as well as TV shows like "Baywatch", "Seinfeld", and "In Living Color."

Debbie was also an activist for little people in Hollywood, making sure they were credited properly for roles, and didn't only get cast in costumed roles, emphasizing their size. Unfortunately, she passed away in 2018 at 58 years old due to health complications.

Loss Of Leg Didn't Keep Her From Romance

On April 3, 2000, People Magazine did another story about Heather Mills whose story first appeared in 1999. It was about the romance between Paul McCartney still grieving over the loss of his wife Linda, and his new romance with British model/activist Heather Mills.

It was not only the 25-year age difference but the fact that Heather had a prosthetic left leg due to being run down in August of 1993 by a speeding police motorcycle, a story I mentioned earlier in this book.

Previous to that she had been a successful swimwear model and only a year after her terrible accident she formed the Heather Mills Health Trust to recycle artificial limbs for land mine victims in war torn nations.

She and Paul met briefly at an event where they were both presenting charitable awards to an animal rights activist who had lost her arms and legs to meningitis. Paul reached out to Heather some weeks afterwards and made a large donation to her charity.

Heather wound up calling off her engagement to another man just two weeks before their wedding. For many people the loss of a limb might be interpreted as having to stay single, but not for Heather Mills. It also says a lot for Paul McCartney.

The World's Only Deaf Solo Percussionist

The year 2000 seems to have been a banner year for articles on people who overcame major obstacles. Evelyn Glennie from Scotland is the world's only classical solo percussionist. As if that wasn't enough on its own, she's also totally deaf.

She started losing her hearing at the tender age of 8, and by 12 was profoundly deaf and had to read lips. It was then that she started percussion lessons. She says she feels the sound with her whole body.

Her teacher would play notes on a timpani drum, while she'd stand with her hands on the wall feeling the vibrations and distinguishing the pitch by where she felt the sound on her body.

It's one of the reasons she performs barefoot. Her own husband was quoted as saying "No one really understands how Evelyn does what she does." She also collects instruments and has more than 1300 of them in her home in England as of the 2000 write-up. She also designs her own line of cymbals.

She's active in the Beethoven Fund, a London-based group that provides music therapy to hearing-impaired children, and in the year the article I read was written, she was in New York City to play six concerts at Avery Fisher Hall in Lincoln Center.

Still very active today she has performed internationally with a wide variety of orchestras and in 2015 she was selected as one of the two laureates for the Polar Music Prize, a Swedish international award started in 1989, and awarded to musicians like Paul McCartney. (My third McCartney reference! LOL)

Penthouse Pet Fights Cancer

Next in the year 2000 is a woman named Leslie Glass. Leslie was a 1994 Penthouse Pet of the Year first runner up. She was a nude model and dancer and was stricken with liver cancer and told she had only weeks to live. She was found to have had 72 tumors in her liver.

Though she lost all her hair with chemo and radiation she was able to make remarkable progress, enough so that she was able to keep dancing, modeling and had a new shoot planned for Penthouse, but also worked with homeless and abused animals and started a charity called Pets for Pets.

Doctors were amazed at her ability to look good and keep working despite the severity of her illness. She described herself as a "Spiritual person" and believes that her good karma had helped her in her fight against the disease.

One of her last events was at a nightclub in New York City. The event was called "Penthouse Pets Bare Their Breasts To Fight Breast Cancer" and it was to benefit the Kathy Keeton Foundation. Kathy was Penthouse publisher Bob Guccione's wife, who passed away from breast cancer in 1997.

When only given two weeks to live from the time of her diagnosis, through her inner strength and perseverance, Leslie was able to make it another six months from the time the article about her was written, and she passed away in August of the year 2000 at the age of 36.

CHAPTER 3

Shooting Victim, Car Crash, Surgery— Nothing Stops This Woman

In 1994 38-year-old golfer Kim Williams was walking into an Ohio drugstore when she was shot in the neck by a stray bullet. It turns out it was fired by a target shooter a half mile away, and was a total accident.

The bullet entered the left side of her neck and lodged below her right collar bone. Luckily it missed all of her major arteries and she was back on the Ladies Professional Golf Association (LPGA) tour in eight days.

Truly a bizarre accident. If she had been a moment earlier or later it might not have happened, or it could have killed her. A fraction of an inch, or a second in time can make a huge difference in a person's life.

Every time you leave your house and choose to go either left or right your whole life will be different. One way something great could happen and the other way something terrible could happen, but you can't think about it too much or you'd become catatonic and never go anywhere. The way you go is the way you were supposed to go. That is your path.

Kim said she had gone to the store to buy some baby oil which she used on her putter to prevent rust.

Eight days later she tied for 10th in the Jamie Farr Toledo Classic. She later had to have an operation to remove the bullet, which was followed by a ruptured disk that also required surgery.

Then in 2001, when the article was written, she had just shot a 72 in the LPGA's first event of that year, when an oncoming car suddenly swerved into her lane and hit her head on. She said the next thing she remembered was waking up in Orlando Regional Medical Center with the policeman who accompanied her there telling her, "I can't believe you're alive."

Among other injuries she had a broken collar bone, and a damaged knee that required surgery. Her Dad said she was like a cat with nine lives but warned her against using them up.

She herself said "I've seen people really suffer. What's happened to me is small by comparison." She went on to say, "I'm doing what I love to do, and whatever problems I had, I'm recovering."

After the crash when doctors told her she wouldn't be able to play for eight weeks, she proved them wrong by being back in four weeks, although she also wound up needing unrelated abdominal surgery.

Friends and family credit her remarkable spirit in being able to recover from so many serious things. She describes herself by saying, "I'm very focused and very intense."

She left the LPGA in 2012 after 25 years of being on tour and now teaches golf to people of all ages.

Film Director Beaten, Needing Brain Surgery Finds Success

Jill Sprecher grew up in Wisconsin and wasn't used to New York ways when in 1985 while working as a waitress, and pursuing a Master's degree in film at NYU, she was the victim of a push in robbery at her apartment in Harlem.

She was thrown to the ground and robbed, and fortunately neighbors held the perpetrator until the police arrived.

Only three months later she was walking near the Port Authority terminal when she was hit in the head with a bottle that was thrown at her, landing her in the hospital needing brain surgery. She had a big blood clot on her brain.

She said she woke up two days later with a shaved head, and her mother standing at her bedside with a wig she had brought from home.

She said she spent a year after that attack having crying spells. Most people would have left and went back to Wisconsin but not Jill. A short time later she suffered yet another assault on the subway when a stranger slapped her in the head for no reason at all.

In 1997 she had had some success with an indie film she wrote with her sister called "Clockwatchers" and then in 2001 she used her terrible experiences to write the film "Thirteen Conversations About One Thing."

With the help of the director of "Clockwatchers" and Michael Stipe from R.E.M. she was able to assemble an all-star cast including Matthew McConaughey, John Turturro, Amy Irving and Alan Arkin.

The film was a hit at the Tribeca Film Festival and won a couple of awards, despite leaving her and her sister $150,000. in debt.

However, she completed her studies and got her Master's in Media Studies and went on to produce and direct films and TV shows, a great example of overcoming obstacles that would have easily stopped many other people.

Not Only Short People Get Bullied

In 2001 a 13-year-old boy named Christopher Velazquez was written about in the New York Post for being bullied so badly in school that in a rare move, school officials agreed to provide him with a bodyguard. He was 6-foot-9, and still growing.

He was afraid to return to school after being beaten and bullied in the gym over a three-day period by kids who were tormenting him because of his size. I'm sure if he had wanted to he could have picked them up and thrown them across the gym, but I guess he was one of those gentle giants you hear about every so often.

The point is that kids can be so mean. Why is that? In one of my last books, I wrote a lot about "Heart Wounds" caused by people being mean to us, and you can be sure that this experience will be with Christopher for the rest of his life.

When he thinks about his childhood, he'll always remember that experience. And as a 6-foot-9 man I'd like to see who comes up to make fun of him then!

Most of these jerks are nothing but bullies! Another student had actually threatened him with a knife, and all for being so tall. As if he had anything to do with his genetics!

What I found most interesting was that there was a photo of him with his parents and his Dad looked even taller than he was, so I guess he could offer some good advice, … or some good martial arts training!

CHAPTER 4

From The Year 2002

He Became A Doctor, An Athlete And A Singer, ... With No Legs

In 2002 an article came out about a man named Ronan Tynan that simply astonished me. Ronan was born in Kilkenny, Ireland with a condition known as bilateral phocomelia, a rare birth defect in which the bones of the lower legs don't grow, leading to deformed feet and legs.

He was born a twin and his twin had the same disability but died at 11 months old from pneumonia. As a teen Ronan was fitted for artificial limbs, but was always told by his father that he could still do whatever he wanted to do.

He grew up on a farm and would help his father attach their 80 cows to milking machines.

He began riding horses and motorbikes. Then at age 20 he had a severe motorbike accident which led to him having his legs amputated below the knee.

He had also damaged his back severely in the accident, and to avoid being confined to a wheelchair, because he would no longer be able to use his prosthetic limbs, he had to have his legs amputated.

But that didn't stop him. He got new prosthetics that helped to straighten his spine, and with the constant encouragement from his father, 18 months later he began competing in the Paralympics and World Amputee Games, and wound up winning 18 gold medals in 8 years in events like the shot put and the long jump.

As if that wasn't enough, he became the first person with a disability to be admitted to the National College of Physical Education in Ireland. He spent two years working in the prosthetics field, and then went on to Trinity College to become a physician specializing in Orthopedic Sports Injuries, and graduated in 1993.

But that's not all. His father also encouraged him to study voice enabling him to win a series of voice competitions including one on a BBC talent show. He studied opera in Germany and England and four years later wound up with a recording contract.

His first album, which went platinum was simply called "Ronan Tynon" after which he became one of the Irish Tenors, a trio that had sold more than one million albums by the time this article had come out in 2002.

Ronan also performed for Pres. Bush and sang at the request of Archbishop Timothy Dolan at St. Patrick's Cathedral in New York City, and he's still actively singing and performing today in 2021.

He Literally Crawled For Miles To Make A Sale

Some salesmen are very persistent, and some would basically do anything to make a sale, but Bill Porter is in a class of his own. Bill Porter was born in San Francisco in 1932 with cerebral palsy, the only child of a housewife and a salesclerk. His disability left him with a twisted right side and slurred speech.

His mother was always very positive and didn't let him dwell on his disability. When he was 17, she enrolled him in public high school and when he graduated his father insisted he get a job, which was not that easy.

He went to an employment agency but after four months of daily rejections the agency suggested he just go home and apply for welfare. That didn't sit well with Bill, so he combed the want ads for himself, and eventually applied for a door-to-door sales job with a company called Watkins, the nation's oldest door-to-door sales company.

They agreed to give him a chance but gave him the worst territory. He had to wake up at 4:45 every morning, because it took him at least 90 minutes to dress himself, and then he had to take two buses to get to his West Portland, Oregon sales territory by 9 A.M.

After a year he began winning sales awards. His boss said that nothing could dampen his enthusiasm and that he never took rejection personally. If people slammed the door on him his mantra was, "The next customer will say yes."

His boss described him as relentless and irresistible. His territory consisted of a 7 mile stretch and once during an ice storm he literally crawled the last part of his route on his hands and knees. He stayed living with his mother until she had to go into a nursing home in the mid-80's. His father had passed away in 1962.

In 1985 he hired an assistant and housekeeper named Shelly Brady, a young mother who worked with him for many years. His mother succumbed to Alzheimer's in 1989, and then in 1993 he needed back surgery, which left him without income and no way to pay his mortgage.

Shelly and her husband got up enough money to buy his house and rented it back to him for a very low rent. His story was so compelling that in 1995, an Oregon based newspaper did a series of feature stories about him.

That led to the TV show 20/20 doing a piece on him in 1998, which led to invitations from major corporations like Amway and Nike to become a motivational speaker and in 2002, the year of the article I read, a TV movie came out about his life called "Door to Door" with Bill Macy, who also co-wrote the script, playing him.

Shelly Brady was so inspired by him that she wrote a book called "Ten Things I Learned From Bill Porter." Unfortunately, he passed away on Dec. 3, of 2013 at the age of 81.

It's described as a personal tale of quiet hero-ism and private victories. Bill Porter was quoted as saying, "I never did anything heroic. I had to pay the rent."

The Paraplegic Who Went To Harvard

In 1990, Brooke Ellison was only 11 years old. It was her first day of junior high school and on her way home she was hit by a car. The damage was devastating, and she was left paralyzed from the neck down. She was a quadriplegic at 11 years old, needing a ventilator to help her breathe.

Her Mom Jean Ellison was determined to help her in any way she could and devoted her life to doing so. Confined to a wheelchair, Brooke graduated from high school with high honors and was accepted by Harvard.

Her mother attended with her to assist in all the things she was not capable of doing, which was most everything. When asked what it was like for Brooke to get through Harvard, her Mom said, "Try to imagine being in a chair with your feet bound, and your hands tied behind your back. Then imagine being on a machine that gives you only 13 breaths per minute. Then imagine never being able to use the bathroom, or the shower when you want to, to brush your teeth, feed yourself, scratch an itch, or wipe your eyes if you need to cry."

"Imagine never having any privacy, not being able to be physically intimate with anyone, or never being able to hug someone when you really want to. Then compound that with sleepless nights when you are unable to breathe, and have wheelchair malfunctions that leave you stranded in bed."

"Then put yourself in one of the most rigorous academic settings in the world, and ask yourself to read thousands of pages of text without being able to turn the pages, attend lectures, seminars and labs in all kinds of weather, study, prepare papers, take tests, and on top of everything else do an original research thesis, submit it on time and have to defend it."

I have to confess to my readers that just writing this story was incredibly moving to me, to see the devotion of her Mom and the determination of Brooke.

She became the very first quadriplegic to graduate from Harvard, but that's not all. She graduated Summa Cum Laude with a Bachelor of Science degree in cognitive neuroscience.

She was written about in the NY Post in 2002 for her book "Miracles Happen– One Mother, One Daughter, One Journey."

Her story was turned into a movie in 2004 called "The Brooke Ellison" story, directed by fellow paraplegic, Christopher Reeve, who I happened to have met before his accident, at a NYC restaurant where we used to hang out.

It was his final project and unfortunately the film wound up airing after his passing.

In 2006 Brooke ran for New York State Senate but was defeated. She is a big supporter and very involved in embryonic stem cell research.

Today she is 41 years old and an Associate Professor at Stony Brook University. She went on to get a Master's degree in Public Policy from the Harvard Kennedy School in 2004, and got her PhD in Sociology from Stony Brook in 2012.

From 2007–2014 she served on the Empire State Stem Cell Board, which designed New York State's stem cell policy. She has taught classes at the undergraduate, Master's, MD and PhD levels, and focuses on medical ethics, science ethics, and health policy.

In 2017 she was chosen to serve on the Board of Directors of the New York Civil Liberties Union, and in 2018 she was chosen to be a Truman National Security Project Partner. On top of everything else she is also a motivational speaker.

I'm sure she is very effective at motivating people. I attended a conference of motivational speakers, many of whom have overcome things like loss of limbs, disfigurement by fire and other types of accidents and things that might stop most people, and the lesson is always the same, ... that self-pity is a terrible thing.

A Paraplegic Who Dances

Kitty Lunn, from New Orleans, started dancing at 8 years old. As a teen she danced principal roles with the National Ballet. In 1967 she moved to New York City and as she was preparing for her Broadway debut, she slipped on the ice, and fell down a flight of stairs breaking her neck and back leaving her a paraplegic.

She spent three years in the hospital enduring five spinal surgeries supported by the boyfriend she went on to marry. Confined to a wheelchair she was determined to continue dancing.

She showed up at dance class where sadly according to her, she was not always made to feel welcome. She managed to develop a way of dancing in her lightweight wheelchair, and in 1995 she founded the Infinity Dance Theatre, an ensemble of dancers with and without disabilities.

Her style is founded in classical ballet, but incorporates jazz and modern dance techniques, which she modifies for her dancers, often shifting the movements from the legs to the arms, while spinning in her chair.

She even got her husband into the act, actor Andrew MacMillan, who designed her lightweight chair, and has performed with her on stage.

Kitty and her troupe perform all over the world. She has become an activist for the disabled and is also an actor who had a recurring role as Sally Horton, a disabled character on the legendary soap opera "As The World Turns."

Kitty also performed at the Alliance Theatre and at the Kennedy Center. She teaches dance for people with disabilities and I'm happy to say that at 70 years old she's still going strong.

The NY Post article in 2002 was due to the fact that she had been nominated for a NY Post Liberty

Medal! As an activist she served on the Performers with Disabilities committees for both Actor's Equity and SAG-AFTRA, the two main entertainment unions, leading negotiations for better use of performers with disabilities.

From Wheelchair To Nascar Rookie

Kelly Sutton was drawn to racing from the time she was a toddler. Her Dad, a now retired police officer was an amateur racer and kept a race car at the house. As a toddler she'd stand on a milk crate to look under the hood.

By 3 years old she was helping to clean mud off the cars, by 10 was racing a motorcycle, and by 12 was racing a go-cart. She said it made her feel "cool."

She also played ball and at 15 years old started experiencing unusual symptoms, like running flatfooted on the field, and feeling extreme fatigue. Her doctor at the time blamed it on adolescence and a cry for attention.

He kept saying the same thing for the next year as her symptoms worsened and it wasn't until her right side went numb that they diagnosed her with

Multiple Sclerosis, a disease that leads to weakening of the muscles and often a life in a wheelchair.

By the age of 18 she was confined to a wheelchair. At age 19 and pregnant in her first marriage, the birth of her daughter triggered a severe flare-up of the disease and she wound up even worse, completely devastated.

Her family vowed to support her through this ordeal, and her Dad asked her if she still wanted to race. As an inspiration to her he bought a small black Ford Pinto, which he converted into a race car to be used by Kelly as an incentive to get better.

She began a grueling exercise program combined with a high protein diet, and an anti-MS drug which she injected herself with daily.

Strictly through perseverance she was racing again by 1993, at 22 years old, and she was winning too! But in 1995 she had a severe car accident after skidding on ice and smashing into a tree.

The injuries which were several broken ribs, a collapsed lung, and a dislocated hip and shoulder led to her worst MS attack to date, plus strained her second marriage at that point, which led to another divorce.

This time her father built her a stationary race car that doubled as a workout machine. This man was amazing. Within two years she was racing again and even picked up a sponsor in the year 2000.

The sponsor was Teva Pharmaceuticals, the company that made the drug she was taking to help prevent relapses. She went on to have a third husband and they are raising their two daughters.

At the time of the writing of the article I read she was going after Rookie of the Year honors in the Nascar Goody's Dash series. She said she "loves to be in control of something that's on the verge of being out of control," and that speed is her passion.

Her last race was in June of 2007 when she finished 20th at the Toyota Tundra Milwaukee 200, and in 2013 she was critically injured in a motorcycle accident while riding as a passenger. Amazingly she recovered after a lengthy rehabilitation.

As many people do who have fought so hard to overcome these huge obstacles in their lives, she has become a motivational speaker, and makes appearances to give hope to other MS sufferers.

Overcoming Nightmarish Childhood To Become A Best Seller

Many people who overcome huge obstacles in their lives go on to either become motivational speakers, write books, or have movies made about their stories because they're so inspirational, and in doing so they tell other people facing adversity that they can do the same thing.

Such is the case of Augusten Burroughs, born Christopher Richter Robinson, who according to the 2002 story about him in People Magazine endured a childhood of madness, abandonment and sexual molestation.

He was the younger of two sons born to his mother a poet, and his father the former head of the philosophy department at the University of Massachusetts Amherst.

At 13 his older brother had already fled their home, and his parents had divorced. His mother, who had a history of mental illness and psychosis gave him to her psychiatrist by signing over guardianship.

The household turned out to be very bizarre with the doctor claiming he could divine the future by examining his own excrement, which is yet another story that disturbs me to even write, and it went downhill from there. The other examples I'll leave out, because no one should have those images in their mind.

The doctor also believed that children became adults at 13 and allowed him to drop out of school in the 6th grade. At 17 he fled that living arrangement, got his own apartment, and earned a GED.

At 18 he changed his name to Augusten Burroughs. His 20's were lost in a sea of alcohol and drugs, but by 30 when he got sober, he began to write.

And as of the writing of this article he wrote about his childhood experiences in a book called "Running With Scissors", which hit No. 5 on the New York Times bestseller list. The book was made into a movie in later years, and he's been writing books ever since. He's also very active in the LGBTQ community as an activist.

From Harvard To Homeless And Back Again

In 1987 Macy DeLong was a married woman working as a biological researcher at Harvard University, where she ran a lab of 25 people, and was living in a comfortable home in Lexington, Massachusetts.

However, during the winter of 1988, she was looking for a warm place to sleep on the street as she willingly left her home and her husband to become homeless.

At the time she had not yet been diagnosed as bipolar but was despondent over not being able to have a child, after suffering through an ectopic pregnancy and two failed rounds of in vitro fertilization.

A suicide attempt landed her in the hospital for three months, and she was released with a prescription for anti-depressants. In the People Magazine article I read she was quoted as saying, "I went from overseeing a lab of 25 people to not being able to tell someone how to wash a test tube without having a panic attack." She became completely dysfunctional.

That was when she left Harvard to begin her six months of homelessness, despite offers of help from her husband and family. She slept on subway gratings, in her car, and even in a cemetery, and got her meals at community centers.

When she told them she was a Harvard biologist they just assumed she was delusional and treated her in a demeaning manner.

She experienced everything that homeless people had to endure from dangerous shelters to indifferent doctors, and she said that no one offered her any kind of real opportunities like a job, or permanent housing. Her first night in the shelter she was robbed at knifepoint of her shoes and I.D.

Amazingly in 1989, while still on the street herself she launched a non-profit agency called "Solutions at Work" that provides homeless people with transitional employment, low-cost moving services, free cars, furniture and clothing.

Shortly afterwards she returned home only to divorce her husband. She used part of her divorce settlement plus $20,000. from her Harvard retirement fund to take over a city-run furniture bank for the poor when she learned it was about to close. She expanded it to include a clothing exchange and moving company.

She estimated that by the time of the writing of the article I referenced, her agency had helped nearly 65,000 people since its inception.

For the next nine years she pursued her mission, and it wasn't until 1998 that she was formally diagnosed as being bipolar and given appropriate medication. Her non-profit agency continued doing well, and as of the writing of this article had an annual budget of $500,000. funded by government grants and private donations.

She once held a dinner at her home made up of Harvard colleagues and homeless people. The women didn't mix too well but the men did okay talking about baseball.

Solutions at Work is still going strong today. Their entire staff and two board members have experienced homelessness.

From The Hood To The Grammys

Eve Jihan Jeffers Cooper, or just Eve as she's known now, was born in the hood in Philly, in 1978 and raised by a single Mom. She says she has no relationship with her Dad who never married her Mom. She was raised in the Philadelphia projects.

Growing up she sang in choirs, and rapped with an all-girls group called Dope Girl Posse. After that group broke up, she went on a solo career as "Eve of Destruction." She even worked as a stripper for a month when she was 18 and said she doesn't regret it. Rapper Mase helped to talk her out of that life.

She rose out of her meager background to be known just as Eve, and became an award-winning rapper, singer, and actress, having released four studio albums, and won a Grammy, a BET Award, an MTV Video Music Award, a Teen Choice Award, and a Washington D.C. Area Film Critics Association Award. She was also ranked number 46 on VH1's list of the 50 Greatest Hip Hop Artists.

At the time of this People article in 2002 she had just done a duet with Alicia Keys in a song called "Gangsta Lovin", and was just 23 years old.

She had also just released a new CD called "Eve-Olution", and had a small part in Ice Cube's movie "Barbershop." Eve went on to reprise that role as Terri Jones in "Barbershop 2: Back in Business", and "Barbershop: The Next Cut."

In 2001 she went on to win a Grammy for the song "Let Me Blow Your Mind", which she sang in a duet with Gwen Stefani.

Known also for her role as Shelley Williams on the UPN sitcom "Eve", she also appeared in several other films. Since 2017 she's been one of the hosts of the CBS daytime talk show The Talk, and had a clothing line called Fetish from 2003 to 2009.

She's graced the covers of several magazines including Rolling Stone, Essence, Vibe, Teen People and more, has appeared in commercials and music videos working with people like Ludacris and Swizz Beatz, and despite the fact that she never thought she'd get married, in 2014 she married British producer and director Maximillion Cooper in Ibiza, Spain after four years of dating.

Now she divides her time between London, Los Angeles and New York and I think you can say she's the perfect example of what you can achieve if you know you have talent and are willing to work hard.

A Modern-Day Harriet Tubman

By the time Susan Burton got her article in People Magazine she had been to prison six times within 16 years and five of those times, when released, she didn't get past the bus terminal where they let her off before succumbing to her old ways.

Susan had a very hard childhood growing up in public housing in East L.A. Molested at 4 by an aunt's boyfriend and gang raped at 14 leading to the birth of her daughter didn't exactly give her a good start on life.

Not surprisingly her father was an abusive alcoholic, and she began drinking at age 12. By 13 she was abusing pills, and after she had her daughter who she wound up leaving with her mother, she hit the streets and for the next five years worked as a prostitute, and then became the mistress to a drug dealer.

When they broke up in 1983, she turned to crime to support her cocaine habit, which led to her first arrest. She was in and out of prison until 1997 when she willingly entered a drug treatment facility and got sober using the 12 steps. She stayed there for 98 days.

She was quoted as saying, "That's all I needed to give me the foundation to rebuild my life, and to do the same for others."

Many former drug and alcohol abusers go on to become counselors in their desire to give back because they are so grateful for having changed their lives, but Susan took it one step further.

For the next two years after she got clean, she worked as a caretaker for the elderly and saved all her money to afford a down payment on her home.

Then she set about healing the relationship with her daughter, who today is very proud of her.

She bought a modest three-bedroom bunga-low in Watts and in 1999 started her non-profit program called *A New Way of Life*. Anywhere from 8-10 parolees at a time were chosen by her to share the house until they could get back on their feet.

Susan insists they go to 12 step meetings, undergo periodic drug tests, and either work or go to school. Eventually each woman is expected to contribute $400. a month to the upkeep of the house.

As of the writing of the People Magazine article I read, she had already helped 82 women, most of whom had been referred by public agencies, and two-thirds of the women have managed to stay straight.

In 2018, the L.A. Times did a follow up story on Susan, and by this time she had helped approximately 1,000 women break the cycle and avoid going back to prison.

She wrote a memoir with a co-writer entitled "Becoming Mrs. Burton: From Prison to Recovery to Leading the Fight for Incarcerated Women" telling her story of terrible violence and abuse which she says is so common amongst incarcerated women.

She went back to Chino Prison that year where she had spent four of her six prison terms to speak to the women and sign copies of her book. She is very active in the criminal justice reform movement.

Her book tour took her to cities and prisons across the country, and she also made the late-night TV and radio circuit. That first house she opened has grown to five homes, and her staff of 25 includes attorneys, social workers, public policy advisors, and people working on political issues. She's trying to get ex-felons the right to vote again.

Supporters have called her a modern-day Harriet Tubman and to that she was quoted as saying, "I try to be humble, but I feel like I'm building an underground railroad!"

CHAPTER 5

From The Year 2003

From Hand Loss To Spinal Surgeon

All of the stories in this book blow me away to use a colloquial expression, but this one has many levels and is purely a miracle. Woosik Chung was born in Korea and as a 3-year-old in 1978, playing hide-and-seek with some friends, he chose to hide behind a tractor whose engine was running.

The little 3-year-old boy reached out to touch the whirring engine and within seconds both of his hands were severed at the wrists. Both hands were laying on the ground and his right thumb had also been cut off.

Seeing the horrifying scene from his window his father ran out with a bucket of ice, and he and his wife carried their son to a hospital a few blocks away, but it was a national holiday in Korea and there were no specialists to be found.

The first part of the miracle is that the father just happened to be an army surgeon, but he had never done any kind of surgery like this before. The article doesn't say how he did it, but it's lucky that it didn't happen here, because in this country unless you have hospital privileges no surgeon can just walk into a hospital and request to do surgery on someone.

But in this case, possibly due to the circumstances and the fact that it was a small child, the father, with the help of his wife who just happened to be a nurse, and the hospital staff re-attached his son's hands by himself in a 9 hour plus operation.

The father was quoted as saying, "I just prayed to G-d and did my best." Well, his best turned out to be amazing. The casts were on for two months and when they were taken off Woosik was not able to move his hands, but he did regain full usage of them a couple of years later, due to the second miracle.

The little boy's grandfather just happened to be a Tae Kwon Do Grand Master. Tae Kwon Do is the Korean style of martial arts. His grandfather used the study of Tae Kwon Do as Woosik's only form of physical therapy.

He trained his grandson for several hours every day, which must have been incredibly difficult for the young boy, but not only did it give him his manual dexterity back, but he also became a black belt in Tae Kwon Do.

Again, because children all over the world can be so cruel, the scars on his wrists brought taunting from his classmates who called him Frankenstein, and when he was 7 and the family moved from Korea to the African nation of Malawi he said he got into fights every day with kids that tormented him.

Finally at 14 he and his family moved to the United States where he attended an elite New Jersey boarding school. Then he went on to Yale University where he also became a Tae Kwon Do champion and was ranked second in the United States in his weight class.

In 1997 he earned a degree in molecular biophysics and was considering trying out for the 2000 Olympics in martial arts, but decided to go to medical school instead. His father, needless to say, was thrilled.

He received his medical degree from the New Jersey Medical School in Newark, and went on to do his residency at Columbia-Presbyterian Hospital in New York City.

Working in New York at Columbia-Presbyterian Medical Center one of the orthopedic surgeons said about him, "Even as a first-year student, he had skills equivalent to someone with six years of experience."

In 2003, the year that the article I read came out in People Magazine, he was in the midst of a five-year surgical residency and had planned to become a hand surgeon when he was finished. He said that was the best way he could ever thank his Dad, by helping others in similar situations.

As an adult his scars are barely noticeable, and his professors only found out about his miraculous story and recovery when he had to write an essay for the residency program at Columbia Presbyterian.

He went on to undertake an orthopedic spine surgery fellowship training at the Emory University Spine Center in Atlanta, Georgia, after which he became board-certified.

He is now the director of spinal surgery at Presbyterian/St. Luke's Medical Center in Denver, Colorado where he focuses on degenerative spine disorders, and treats spinal disorders in athletes, as well as arthritic spines, spinal tumors, spinal infections and trauma. He's also been featured on Good Morning America!

Not to take away from this incredible miracle, or make light of the subject, but because life often imitates art, and because I am also a comedy writer, I wonder if he ever read my Weekly World News article entitled, "College Professor Fired for Casually Removing His Spine in Class", and if not, I wonder whether I should send it to him! (LOL)

It's just one of the fun, bizarre stories in my absurdist book called "Man Robs Bank With His Chin."

https://www.amazon.com/dp/1735442623

The story goes that due to a severe car accident college professor Herb Sturm was left with a removable spine. Ever since he recovered, while teaching Invertebrate Zoology of all things, he would casually reach behind himself, whip out his spine and slump to the ground in a pile of clothing. Then he would ask his students to help him reinsert his spine.

The students rebelled and said at first, they thought it might have been an accident, which was Sturm's claim, but eventually they realized he was doing it on purpose. And they complained that they were nervous to help him re-insert his spine, because "What if it goes in wrong, and something really bad happens?"

Anyway, in case you enjoy absurdist humor and that story interests you, and you want to find out how it ended up feel free to contact me at Jeffrey@jeffreygurian.com to order a signed paperback copy or an e-version of the book! Or you can just go to Amazon which is probably a lot easier! **https://www.amazon.com/dp/1735442623**

<u>Overcoming Chronic Pain</u>

In 2003, People Magazine chronicled the account of Hannah Terrell a 20-year-old Chagrin Falls, Ohio woman who had been living in intractable pain since she was 10 as the result of a 15-foot fall from a zip line that was strung between two trees in her backyard.

After enduring five surgeries to try and fix her shattered ankle, nerve damage set in and the pain had gotten so bad that there were times she could not stand up for more than a few minutes.

She was crying all the time and had to miss many classes. Luckily, she was able to connect with Dr. Edward Covington, director of the Cleveland Clinic Pain Program who at the time was one of the very few M.D.'s in the country to work with people in intractable pain, using not only pharmaceuticals but also exercise, biofeedback, self-hypnosis, psychological counseling and family therapy.

That work is based on scientific research showing that pain is affected by emotions, fears and beliefs. Dr. Covington explained that "treating pain as a mere symptom is not always enough."

As a last resort, Hannah agreed to try this therapy at the Cleveland Clinic, which offers a three to four week course to a dozen pain sufferers at a time.

At the clinic they learn to modify the mind-body phenomenon of pain with psychological or external events, such as jogging, swimming, lifting weights, punching a heavy bag, and yoga, which began to eliminate her fear of being able to do these things without an increase in pain.

It allows people to think that maybe they're not as helpless as they thought they were. After three weeks she was discharged to go back to school, and has been using the techniques she learned to manage her pain and become more social.

The article said she's standing and attending parties again, and has even been able to dance. She was quoted as saying, "It's nice to feel a little bit normal again."

Small But Huge

This story in particular is very special to me because I happen to know the person it's about personally. You may not know him personally, but I bet that you know of him.

It was in 2003 that Peter Dinklage hit stardom. He had just finished starring in the indie-comic film which wowed people at Sundance entitled "The Station Agent" in which his 4'6" stature caused by dwarfism was not the point of his role.

He played a lonely station agent named Finbar McBride who was working as a trainspotter, and in this movie he actually gets the girl. In this film there were two women that were taken with him, played by Patricia Clarkson, and Michelle Williams.

It was a complete disconnect from the type of parts that little people usually get cast in.

There was a great two-page article in the New York Post about him in which he was quoted as saying about most parts for little people, "What irritates me most about dwarf parts is the cuteness. I don't like the parts that make us angelic. Because you don't end up with the girl, you're left in the dark and the cold."

As a kid in school, he was tortured by other kids using references that compared him to Herve Villechaize, at the time the best-known dwarf for his role as Tattoo, in the TV show Fantasy Island starring Ricardo Montalban. Tattoo's iconic line was "Ze plane, ze plane" as he spotted people flying in on planes to live out their fantasies.

In an upcoming movie called *"Tiptoes"* Peter is cast as a drunken, drugged out bad boy who shares sex scenes with Patricia Arquette, a movie supposedly loosely based on the life of Herve Villechaize who was only 3'11" tall.

Herve wound up committing suicide 10 years after Fantasy Island ended when he was reduced to doing commercials for Dunkin' Donuts pointing at the counter and ordering "Ze plain, ze plain"! Sadly, he shot himself in the head.

Peter turned down many offers to play an elf in films but took the part of a successful businessman in Will Ferrell's movie "Elf." At the time of this article 17 years ago he was planning on performing at Lincoln Center in a new play about the French painter Toulouse Lautrec, and all the women he had in his life. I think it's safe to say he was definitely "too loose"! (LOL)

And by the way, Toulouse was reported to be anywhere between 4'6" and 4'11".

Lautrec's dwarfism was considered to be a result of his parents being first cousins. At 13 he broke one of his femurs and at 14 broke the other and his legs stopped growing and never healed right. As with most people considered "different" he was tormented by his peers and suffered with alcoholism. He also frequented prostitutes who he felt were the only women who understood him.

I first met Peter at the Naked Angels Theatre in New York City when the acting troupe of the same name had their own place on 17th Street. The Naked Angels is a theatre troupe made up of many performers who went on to become household names like Sarah Jessica Parker, Matthew Broderick, Fisher Stevens, and Marisa Tomei.

In the late 80's and early 90's I used to be one of the writers whose work they would read at an event called Tuesdays at Nine. It's where I got to meet a young Ethan Hawke in 1993 who had just done his first film "Alive", about people who survived a plane crash in the Andes.

In 1992, I asked Peter to star in one of my home-made comedy films that came out of a meeting I had years earlier with Woody Allen.

It was an absurdist film called "Men Who Dance Where They're Not Supposed To" and it was part of a series I made called "The Men Who Series" about men who do very unusual things, like "Men Who Take A Pitchfork To The Movies" and "Men Who Enjoy Latin Dancing With Tools."

In the film Peter gets arrested for dancing in a "No Dancing" zone in Manhattan. The sign clearly says "No Dancing Tuesdays and Thursdays or Any Other Time", but he can't help himself and refuses to obey. In a dramatic scene with an actor from the Troma films he gets arrested and taken away for illegal dancing.

The entire "Men Who" Series is up on my Comedy Matters TV You Tube channel at **https://www.youtube.com/comedymatterstv**

Who knew that some 25 years later Peter Dinklage would become one of the biggest stars in the world for his portrayal of Tyrion Lannister in the blockbuster HBO series *Game of Thrones?* (That's a rhetorical question by the way, meaning it does not require an answer!)

I absolutely love the fact that through his determination Peter has changed the game and destroyed a stereotype. For some reason that means the world to me!

CHAPTER 6

<u>From The Year 2009</u>

<u>83-Year-Old Does Handstand</u>

I was thumbing through the New York Post in April of 2009 when I was struck by a photo of what appeared to be an elderly woman doing a handstand and a yoga pose called the "peacock pose" where she lifts her body off the ground with just her hands, with her legs extended in the air behind her.

At first I thought it was trick photography, but as I read the article, I realized she was really an 83-year-old yoga instructor, and the photos were not CGI. They were real.

And she was wearing a pink jumpsuit and pearls, not workout clothes.

Her name is Bette Calman and she lives in Australia. The London Daily Mail quoted her as saying, "I'm proof that if you keep at it, you'll get there. I can do more now than I could 50 years ago."

At the time the article was written, she had been teaching yoga for 40 years and doing at least 11 classes a week. Her students must have adored her. She said "You're never too old. The body is a remarkable instrument."

Many people use age as an obstacle, which is why I never ask anyone their age or divulge mine. It's very hypothetical. Your age is solely based on whenever your parents decided to try and make a baby, and it could have happened at any time.

As soon as you own an age, you're responsible for it and people expect you to act a certain way correlating with whatever age you claimed. I totally reject that. Your inner child is still alive and well inside of you and needs a big hug every so often to make you feel safe and wanted.

If you remember how exciting it was as a child when your friends came to call for you and ask if you could come out to play, that's not supposed to stop. Just because we grow up and do serious things, we're still supposed to have fun.

If you came to my house, you'd think a child lived with me because it's filled with balloons, crayons, and little toys all over the place. It's my own personal Happiness Center, and I teach people to create their own Happiness Centers in whatever size space they call home.

As soon as you leave the house you're at the mercy of whatever The Universe has in store for you. The only place you can hope to control your environment is where you live, and I feel you should surround yourself with things that make you happy.

Everywhere you look should be something that makes you smile. White makes me happy, so my carpeting is white, my piano is white, most of my furniture is white and my car is white. My apartment is very bright, because I'm sensitive to light. I need a lot of it!

Many people live in dark apartments and wonder why they're depressed.

Anyway, back to Bette Calman, she's also an author who wrote three books, ran yoga centers for three decades and was a constant fixture on TV in Australia.

I looked her up on Google and now at 90 she's still strong and healthy and practicing yoga. She finally retired from teaching at 87, but still does it for herself, proving old age is an obstacle you can overcome.

CHAPTER 7

From The Year 2013

From Kenya To Bed-Stuy Brooklyn

This obstacle was kind of different than all the others I've written about so far, and also appealed to me personally on several levels. It was an article in New York Magazine about a collage artist named Wangechi Mutu from Africa. Kenya to be exact.

The writer said as she entered Wangechi's brownstone in Bed-Stuy Brooklyn, she was struck by the knee-high piles of magazines like Harper's Bazaar, The Source, National Geographic and Vogue.

Right away I felt jealous because I love magazines so much, I had to stop ordering them. I limited myself to only New York Magazine, and People Magazine because I had subscribed to so many that there was tremendous pressure to read all the interesting articles, and in doing so not getting any of my work done.

Somewhere I read an article about other people like myself who were overloaded with interesting magazines, and they were suffering with Depression from the stress of not being able to get to them all.

Once I read that and realized I was not alone I knew what I had to do and since I cancelled all those subscriptions, I am much freer, mentally and physically.

Anyway, Wangechi would cut out images from all of these magazines and separate them into categories like "Jewelry", "Machines", "Legs", "Animals", and "Plants."

When she was a little girl in Kenya her father had subscribed to National Geographic, and she always wondered why the African people were always shown as just tribesmen. She didn't feel that it was an accurate depiction of the life she knew.

She described it as "akin to the Amish becoming the poster children for America."

As she got older her family moved to Nairobi, and her journey to Brooklyn took 41 years.

It involved high school in Wales, college at Cooper Union in New York City, to the very prestigious M.F.A. program at Yale, and then on to Brooklyn where she lives with her husband and two daughters.

From the year 2000 until 2012 she was caught up in a terrible immigration snafu where if she left the country, she wouldn't be allowed back in. Needless to say, she didn't leave and was not able to attend shows in London, Brussels, or Berlin and could not visit her family in Africa.

Her whole experience was evident in her work, and at the time of the writing of the article she was getting ready for her first showing at the Brooklyn Museum which will include her collages, sketches, sculptures, and videos. The retrospective is entitled *The Fantastic Journey*, which I think captures the essence of her story.

Hockey Goalie With M.S.

I don't know much about sports, but I do know that of all the positions in hockey the goalie is a very difficult position, fraught with danger with pucks flying at your head at 100 miles per hour.

Josh Harding was only 28 years old in 2013, living in Minnesota, when the article about him came out in People Magazine.

He was the goalie for the NHL's Minnesota Wild team, and had just been diagnosed with Multiple Sclerosis, a degenerative disease that affects the central nervous system, with the potential of losing all muscle control and even causing blindness.

He feared being restricted to a wheelchair but with early treatment he has become the first professional athlete to compete with M.S., which his neurologist characterized as "amazing!"

Earlier in the year he had complained of neck pains and fatigue and seeing black spots in front of his eyes that interfered with his vision. Then his right leg gave out in practice and doctors discovered lesions in his spinal cord and brain.

At first, he didn't tell anyone. It was too upsetting. His Coach just said, "If you're healthy we're going to play you." And that was a huge relief to him.

At the time of the article, he was still able to skate due to early diagnosis and treatment, and often what can be even more important, a very positive attitude.

I can't stress enough how hard that is to maintain but how important it is to try. We all vibrate at different levels. When you're happy you're vibrating at a high level. When you're sad you're vibrating at a low level and your immune system becomes depleted. When you're positive it strengthens your immune system and helps you fight off whatever is attacking you.

In both of my own hospitalizations for my heart attack and for Covid Double Pneumonia I had to work very hard to stay positive, and the kindness and support I received from so many people really helped in a big way.

In his first game back after his diagnosis he won in a shutout against the opposing team. He wound up winning the Bill Masterton Memorial Trophy, which is awarded annually to the NHL player who best exemplifies the qualities of perseverance, sportsmanship, and dedication to the sport. It's named for the only NHL player in history to have died as the result of injuries suffered during a game.

Josh had to retire after the 2014-2015 season when his MS caused such severe dehydration that he had to be hospitalized, and he left the game he had loved all his life. But what a battle he put up in the meantime.

The last report I found was that as of 2018, he was working as a goalie coach at Edina High School in his hometown.

A Woman With A Big Heart

Angela Redd was a developmental specialist at Blythedale Children's Hospital in Valhalla, New York and had taken care of literally thousands of medically fragile children during her years there.

But one baby, named Saliman stood out to her because he didn't have much attention or many visitors. He was only 2 months old and was suffering from a rare medical condition known as Bartsocas-Papas Syndrome that causes severe physical malformations and disabilities.

He had webbed toes and webbed fingers and tubes running into his body to help him eat and breathe and for some reason Angela felt a strong bond to this infant.

He needed surgeries on his legs, hands and mouth but when she learned that he would be placed in foster care she convinced her husband that they train to become his foster parents. His real parents gave him up because they couldn't take care of him.

Angela was quoted in the People Magazine article as saying, "I don't want anyone else to be his Mom but me." He started getting fitted for prosthetics at 16 months old because he had to have both his legs amputated, and they saw him through years of surgeries, more fittings, and physical, speech and occupational therapy.

They were amazed by his ability to remain cheerful through the whole thing, and what they called his "unbreakable spirit."

He even auditioned for his school play, Guys and Dolls, which was MY high school play. I still remember that I played the part of Rusty Charlie! (LOL)

In 2018 he graduated from high school and was one of the recipients of the John Lepping Memorial Scholarship, which supports disabled youngsters seeking to further their education. That includes students with spinal cord injuries, rare illnesses and syndromes, and Cerebral Palsy.

In the People Magazine article Angela was named one of People's "Heroes." Well deserved!!!

CHAPTER 8

From The Year 2014

The Obstacle Of Hate

I'm writing this book in 2020, but this story was written about in the New York Post in 2014 that actress Tamera Mowry had received incredible online hate for marrying a white man.

She and her identical twin sister had both starred in the ABC sit-com *Sister, Sister* from 1994 to 1999. The show was about twin sisters separated at birth and adopted by different families who just happen to meet when they're 14, and realize that they're sisters.

Tamera and her sister themselves come from an inter-racial marriage.

Tamera had met her husband, Fox News reporter Adam Housley at Pepperdyne College where they both went to school, and they dated for many years before they got married.

Most of the hate came from the Black community who accused her of being a traitor to her race and called her horrible names. She said her marriage was based on pure love and nothing else and that they are raising their kids to just see them as their parents and not one Black and one White. (Capitals are also MY choice!)

The article brought out how this has been happening for years, using Mitt Romney holding his Black adopted grandson in his lap, or Supreme Court Justice Clarence Thomas being accused of being anti-Black, and rejecting the Black race for marrying a White woman.

In an interview with Oprah, Tamera told Oprah that they wouldn't let haters drag them down. A great quote from the article said," Poisonous attempts to shame are an old, endless schoolyard game played by bullies who never grew up and can't stand other people's Happiness or success." (The capital "H" in Happiness is of course mine! LOL)

So "obstacles" don't only have to be physical, or mental impairments. They can also be social obstacles as well, which are just as powerful and often just as hard if not harder to rise above.

No Arms Or Legs Couldn't Stop Him

In this book I've covered several stories of people who had to lose limbs due to accident or illness, but this story is different because the protagonist was born without arms or legs, and never knew what it was like to have either.

Nick Vujicic was born in Melbourne, Australia with a very rare disease called Tetra–Amelia Syndrome, and he said the childhood bullying "made life not worth living."

At ten years of age, he almost committed suicide by allowing himself to slide under the water of his bathtub, but then thought of the sadness it would cause his family and he changed his mind.

Of course the cruel bullying was endless, as it was for most of the stories in this book because there is an element of people who thrive on putting other people down to make themselves feel better about themselves, but I bet it doesn't work. They will always be miserable which is what they deserve.

By his teens he was getting around in a motorized wheelchair controlled with a special joystick, and had lots of friends. He had also already started a career as a motivational speaker. He was an Evangelical Christian and felt strengthened by his faith but was longing for a relationship.

In his People Magazine article in 2014 he was quoted as saying, "The fear of being alone is more disabling than having no arms and legs."

He often found himself wondering "Who would want to marry me?" But then as in a miracle and a gift from G-d during a speaking engagement in Dallas in 2010, he met a beautiful Mexican-Japanese woman who felt drawn to him after hearing him speak.

Her name was Kanae Miyahara, and she was a nursing student who was quoted as saying, "His lack of limbs wasn't something I gave much thought to." What an amazing human being.

In 2011 they got engaged and were married in 2012. They danced at their wedding with Nick in his specialized wheelchair. As of the writing of the article they had one child, a son named Kiyoshi. Now they have four children including a pair of identical twins and reside in Southern California.

On the road, Nick has a caretaker who helps him with things, but he can do a lot on his own. He wiggles in and out of his clothes, brushes his teeth with a wall mounted brush, and can type 43 words a minute with his toes which are attached to his midsection.

Nick has become an internationally known motivational speaker and some five million people have attended his talks. He's also an Evangelist, and a New York Times best-selling author.

His first book, written in 2010, *Life Without Limbs: Inspiration for a Ridiculously Good Life* has been translated into 30 languages. His last book in 2018 is titled *Be The Hands and Feet: Living Out G-d's Love For All His Children,* and he also has a DVD collection for young people entitled *No Arms, No Legs, No Worries.*

So the next time you're in a singles bar feeling sorry for yourself thinking you'll never meet anyone, think of Nick Vujicic, and smile, ... then give yourself a strong dose of hope.

CHAPTER 9

<u>From The Year 2015</u>

<u>The Height Of Cruelty</u>

I think it's safe to say that every single person has something about themselves that they would change if they could. Who is totally 100% happy with their appearance, … although I'm sure you've also had the experience of meeting someone who acted like they took credit for their genetics, as if it was some sort of personal accomplishment.

Those are the obnoxious kind of so-called "beautiful people" that are so taken with themselves, and you just know they think they're something special. Egotistical to the max!

You know how bad you'd feel if the kids in your school made fun of you, or even worse if you were the victim of cyber-bullying which is all too common these days? Well, just try and imagine how you would feel if you were labeled "the ugliest woman in the world" on the internet, where everyone in the world had the opportunity to see it.

Such is the case for a woman named Lizzie Velazquez, who in 2015 was the subject of an article in People Magazine for the documentary made about her called *A Brave Heart; The Lizzie Velazquez Story.*

Lizzie was born with Marfan Syndrome which is a rare genetic disorder that affects the body's connective tissue, which is kind of the body's glue that holds the body's cells, organs and tissues together. It also helps the body grow and develop properly.

Sufferers tend to be tall and often skeletally thin, with distorted facial features. It can also affect the heart and the spine.

When Lizzie was 17, while looking for music on the internet, she happened to stumble across a You Tube video of herself calling her "the ugliest woman in the world", which she said "crushed her spirit."

And how could it not? A native of Austin Texas, her ordeal started when she excitedly started kindergarten and wondered why the other children stared at her and made fun of her.

She said she'd get her confidence back by the end of each school year but then the next year she had to start all over again.

When she found that You Tube video, she said it threw her into a tailspin as there was not even one positive or supportive comment, and it made her think whether she even wanted to bother anymore trying to build back her confidence.

As if the Marfan's wasn't bad enough, she also suffers with something called "lipodystrophy" which makes it very difficult to gain weight. At 25 years old she weighed only 58 pounds.

One day in high school she was asked to share her story at an assembly and discovered her passion for being a motivational speaker. People were drawn to her. She said it took a lot of work and determination, and she started getting speaking invitations from other schools.

Then came her 2013 Ted Talk which garnered over 10 million views. That really raised her profile. As she described it in her People Magazine article, "I was just a girl in her room feeling sorry for herself, and trying to dream of a world where I would be accepted. And now I get to travel the world helping others. It's more than I could ever have dreamed of."

Her fight to get anti-bullying legislation passed in Congress is chronicled in the Brave Heart documentary. She is also the author of 4 books, one called *Dare to Be Kind—How Extraordinary Compassion Can Transform Our World,* and she's now comfortable enough to post photos of herself on Instagram.

Lizzie is certainly a perfect example of what this book is about, overcoming obstacles that could easily stand in your way. Go Lizzie!

Paralyzed Beauty

Lots of girls like to watch make-up videos, and if you watched Jordan Bone's make-up videos you might not even be able to tell she's in a wheelchair. This beautiful girl is a tetraplegic, which usually means the person is paralyzed both in their arms and legs.

In Jordan's case it means she can't move her legs. She can move her arms, just not her hands.

When she was 15 years old, Jordan who lives in Norfolk, England accepted a ride from a 17-year-old, and the car skidded off the road leaving her with a broken neck and severe injuries.

She says she knew right away that she was paralyzed because she couldn't feel her legs. As a child who had loved to dance this was not an easy concept for her to grasp.

While recuperating in the hospital she turned to guided meditation videos on You Tube which she credits for helping her deal with the Depression that followed once she realized that she wasn't going to be able to walk again.

After realizing how much the You Tube videos helped her, she decided to pay it forward and create her own motivational blog and make-up tutorials, which she does on You Tube, and where she currently has 189,000 subscribers.

I watched some of her You Tube videos in which she candidly discusses the accident, and her injuries, and how she needs round the clock caretakers since among other things, she has to be turned periodically to keep her organs functioning properly.

At the time of her People Magazine article in 2015 she was engaged to a guy she met while paralyzed, who was a nutritionist and personal trainer, but in 2017 he broke off their engagement.

I watched another video of hers where she discusses that break up and says she's doing ok with it.

She takes questions from fans and when they asked her what she feels has been her greatest accomplishment, besides learning to apply her make-up by herself, she said it was getting herself off anti-depressants.

She wrote a book about her life called *My Beautiful Struggle,* and in the article, her ending quote was "At the end of the day I just remind myself that I'm grateful to be alive."

Laughter Is Still The Best Medicine

Comedians have a very different way of viewing the world. I know that because I've been involved in that world professionally since 1977.

Many people say that comedians are in truth usually very depressed people. It's true that some comics have difficult backgrounds, which led them to take it to the stage and make audiences laugh at their pain, but Margaret Cho's story took it to a whole other level.

Growing up in San Francisco, she endured sexual abuse at the hands of a family friend from the time she was just 5 years old. At 14 she was raped by someone else she was acquainted with.

The kids at school found out and of course bullied her about it. I'd like to interject here to say that I think that bullying is one of the most important things we have to deal with today. Why are people so cruel?

She hid the abuse from her conservative Korean family for many years, and at 17 dropped out of high school when one of her favorite teachers was killed for being gay.

When she finally opened up to her parents about her history of abuse, they advised her to not say anything about it because of certain "complications" about accusing her abuser.

Like some comics she got the courage to talk about it on stage, the way Maria Bamford discusses her trials with Depression and mental illness in her act.

At the time of Margaret's People Magazine article in 2015 she was getting ready to tape a Showtime special at New York's Gramercy Theatre, a venue I've been to many times for different comedy events.

She talks about wanting to kill every child molester, rapist and animal abuser, and credits the late Joan Rivers, who was a dear friend of mine, and who I used to write for, for inspiring what she calls her "outrageous brand of comedy."

She says it's really hard to shock her, and she was shocked by Joan's comedy. So Margaret actually sings a song in her act called *I Want To Kill My Rapist,* and she says that women in the audience who unfortunately identify scream and cry and sing along.

Her quote on what she does was, "Sharing the suffering alleviates the burden. And that's what I'm trying to do." It's basically what they do in 12 step programs. Sharing from the heart!

The last time I saw Margaret she was appearing in New York headlining at Gotham Comedy Club, one of my home clubs, and she was covered with tattoos. She said it was in response to people bullying her about her weight, and went on to say that the tattoos help celebrate her curvy body. Bravo!!!

Toxic Shock And Loss Of Leg

It was around 2015 when people, especially women became aware of something called Toxic Shock Syndrome, a potentially fatal bacterial infection often associated with tampon usage.

According to the Center for Disease Control it affects 1 in 100,000 women every year. Cases had surfaced in the 80's, which caused tampon boxes to carry warnings telling women to change their tampons every 4-8 hours, and to use the lowest absorbency possible.

It reared its ugly head again when 5'11" runway model Lauren Wasser had to lose her right leg from the knee down, and suffered severe damage to her left foot, requiring amputation of her toes, not to mention the heart attack and gangrene that came with it. She was given a 1% chance of surviving.

It had started with flu-like symptoms, which caused her to leave a birthday party early in 2012 and return to her apartment in Santa Monica to get some sleep.

The next thing she remembers is waking up in the hospital with tubes down her throat after being found unconscious on the floor of her apartment.

Her mother had become worried about not being able to reach her, and had the police check up on her.

She was running 107 fever and experiencing organ shut down, along with excruciating pain. That's where she was diagnosed with Toxic Shock Syndrome despite the fact that she said she had changed her tampon three times that day.

She spent three months in the hospital and another eight months in a wheelchair and said she wanted to kill herself.

Her Mom and younger brother inspired her to carry on, and her best friend who was a photographer and videographer helped her get over her self-consciousness about her prosthetic leg by constantly shooting stills and video of her and showing it to her, until it desensitized her to it.

She wound up suing the tampon manufacturer seeking damages and fighting for clearer instructions on tampon boxes.

At the time of the article, she had just signed with a new modeling agency in Los Angeles, and was working to inspire others with disabilities. She said, "I want kids with amputations to know they're still beautiful. I can turn this into something positive and that's my whole life goal now."

As I often do after writing each of these stories, I look on the internet to see if I can find anything current about each of these inspiring people.

Six years after losing her right leg Lauren wound up having to lose her left leg as well, and now wears two prostheses. She has several sets, often in gold, and there are videos of her running at full speed on the track and on playing fields.

She wore gold running blades to run the NYC marathon. In a TV interview on the Today Show in 2019, the day she was being honored by the Challenged Athlete's Foundation, when asked about her modeling career, she said she was currently signed with Adidas and doing things with H&M.

She was also quoted as saying, "Losing the first leg gave me life, losing the second leg gave me freedom," which she explained was a choice to give herself a better life because she was living with so much pain in her left leg, and she had hit 30 and wanted to become a Mom. She felt it was the best choice she could have made. Such a brave woman!

Down But Still Up

There seem to be varying degrees of Down Syndrome as there are with autism, and a young man named Brandon Gruber of Santa Cruz, California exemplified what is possible to achieve despite having Down Syndrome.

When he first moved there with his parents at 15 years old, he was viciously bullied at school, as is the case with most of the people I've written about in this book.

That's when he decided that Down Syndrome would not define him, and he decided to start a new chapter in his life. That is a very important concept to grasp. He made a decision to make a change in his life and in the way he was being perceived.

So he joined every club he could and "redefined himself." He wound up being crowned "Homecoming King" at Aptos High School and said it was "the happiest thing that ever happened to me."

He felt so grateful that he wanted to do more for other people and formed a non-profit called 321life.com to help other kids less fortunate.

A talented artist in his own right, he found out that some of the students couldn't afford to go to the winter ball and prom, so he raised over $12,000. mostly by selling his own artwork, to send 19 kids to the winter ball and prom, and even bought yearbooks for another 21 kids who would not have been able to afford them.

In 2015 People Magazine wrote about him as one of their "Heroes." When I looked Brandon up on the internet, I found that his 321 non-profit has continued to help people.

He has become very active in the National Down Syndrome Society and has established The Brandon Gruber Scholarship, whose goal is to support self-advocates who wish to pursue their passion for visual and performing arts.

As an accomplished artist himself, he exhibits his own artistic talents by doing gallery displays of his work, modeling, acting and fashion design.

The support he's gotten from his family and community has been invaluable in his ability to accomplish all of these things.

His motto is "Work Hard, Choose Kindness, and Be Yourself." I think kindness is the most important thing in helping people to thrive.

When I was hospitalized with Covid Double Pneumonia, the kindness of the first responders, hospital staff and the literally hundreds and hundreds of people that sent me messages of love and support helped me to get through that ordeal.

It's just too bad that sometimes we have to be in such dire straits before we find out how many people care about us.

At the time of the writing of the People Magazine article his foundation had helped over 500 people. One of my favorite quotes of his is, "I do have limits, but I also have goals and dreams. It's not about Down Syndrome, it's about who you are, not what people think."

There's a great little video about him on You Tube. He's truly inspirational and a great example of what people can accomplish when they put their mind to work and make a decision.

https://youtu.be/nbeSFiCEWQ0sad

He Literally Gave An Arm And A Leg

I think it's safe to say that most people would not be able to withstand the grueling training and rehearsals necessary to be on Dancing With The Stars, no less come in third in the competition.

Now think about doing that with only one arm and one leg. Such was the case with Alabama native Noah Galloway, who was the third amputee to compete on the show after Heather Mills, and Amy Purdee, both of whom as Noah explains have different kind of injuries. He has a prosthetic knee, which makes it even harder to kneel.

The former Army sergeant was injured on Dec. 19th, 2005 in Iraq, when the Humvee he was riding in hit a tripwire that set off a roadside bomb, and the vehicle was blown into a ditch. Noah lost most of his left arm and his left leg above the knee.

When he woke up in Walter Reed Army Medical Hospital in Washington six days later on Christmas Day he was greeted by his parents. His Mom gave him the bad news. The head medic who had treated him thought he would never walk and talk again due to his extreme blood loss.

He adapted quite quickly to a prosthesis and actually walked on it the first day, which amazed the doctors and hospital staff.

Even though people told him to expect a Depression he never thought it would happen to him because he considered himself "an invincible person."

He married his second wife Tracy with whom he has two of his three children, but even with the support of his family he did go into a deep Depression. I always capitalize the word Depression because it's such a powerful force.

He turned to alcohol and often drank alone at home when he wasn't out partying.

And then one day he just decided to turn his life around. He thought about his kids and realized he wasn't being a good father. He also realized that he still had two good limbs.

Having been a runner and fitness trainer, he began a rigorous training schedule that landed him on the cover of Men's Fitness in 2014. He also pushed himself to compete in obstacle course races. In his People Magazine article in 2015 he was quoted as saying, "Everything I do is a struggle because of my injuries. But that motivates me."

It was that cover in Men's Fitness that led the producers of DWTS to invite him to participate in the show. He had never really danced before but is in excellent physical shape, and his determination led him to become an incredible dancer.

His physical strength allowed him to do one-arm lifts with his dancing partner Sharna Burgess, which totally amazed the judges. You can see it on You Tube.

He often performs shirtless which has become a big thing with fans, and he has learned to change his eating habits in order to sculpt his body the way he wants it to look on camera.

He has three children with two wives, and broke off an engagement in 2016 because he felt if he had any more children, he'd be spreading himself too thin and he wanted to be able to be there for the ones he already had.

At the end of the article, he said his next goal was to get a motorcycle, which would require him to get a prosthetic arm. The prosthetic arm would also come in handy allowing him to wear the two leather jackets given to him by Kenneth Cole.

He's gone on to become a motivational speaker, a guest on many TV shows, and has written a memoir called *Living With No Excuses: The Remarkable Rebirth of an American Soldier.* A true hero in anyone's eyes.

CHAPTER 10

From The Year 2016

No Legs To Stand On

This is a book about people overcoming obstacles that would stop most people, and this is a story with not one but two miracles. Jen Bricker grew up in Hardinville, Ill. in the 90's when the most popular thing to do was to go roller skating.

That would have been fine except that she was born with no legs. An amniotic band stopped blood from reaching her lower body while she was still growing inside her Mom. Her parents abandoned her and put her in foster care.

Luckily, she was adopted as an infant, by a wonderful family who already had three sons. Her older brothers and her parents taught her how to navigate the world with confidence despite her condition. They even turned down a school-assigned aide when she was in the second grade to help her become self-sufficient.

She remembers being six the first time she saw U.S. Olympic star gymnast Dominique Moceanu on TV and decided she wanted to be like her. She saw a resemblance in the fact that they looked somewhat alike, were both "tiny", and were both born to Rumanian parents.

She says she was drawn to her but couldn't really say why. When Jennifer was 8, she told her parents she wanted to become a gymnast, so they let her use the trampoline they had in the backyard, and she began collecting trophies in power tumbling. In high school she was the tumbling champion of Illinois.

During the 1996 Olympics she sat glued to the TV watching the 14-year-old Dominique Moceanu perform in her events, and wondered aloud that it would be amazing if they were somehow related.

When Jen was 16 her curiosity got the better of her and she asked her adoptive Mom if she knew what her last name was when she was born. Her mother took out a set of documents she had been keeping all those years and told Jen that she better sit down.

Jen's response was "I'm always sitting down." Her mother showed her that her last name had been Moceanu. She was actually Dominique's sister.

She spent the next four years trying to reach Dominique without any success. Then somehow she managed to get her home address in 2007 and composed a letter explaining who she was.

Two weeks later she received a Christmas card with a letter inside it from Dominique and within the letter was a sentence that said, "You're about to be an auntie", and she said that's when she knew she had been accepted into the family.

They reunited in Cleveland in 2008 and found she also had another sister named Christina who grew up with Dominique. The three women got matching sister tattoos.

At the time of this article in People, Jen had become an aerialist who opened for Britney Spears' Circus Tour, a gymnast, a motivational speaker, and an author. When she feels it's appropriate, she walks on her hands, but most of the time she uses a wheelchair.

In her book *Everything is Possible-Finding The Faith and Courage to Follow Your Dreams,* which became a New York Times best seller, she says finding out her famous surname and that she was Dominique's sister was like finding out she was a princess. She says that Happiness is a choice. She also said she wanted to get married and have kids and adopt a couple more.

In 2019 she got married to Dominik Bauer, in a wedding that was also covered in People Magazine. They met in his hometown in Austria when she was there for a book signing, and he said he was struck right away, especially after he read her book. He knew he had to have her in his life.

After three months of correspondence, they got together in Los Angeles, and he said he didn't tell her for another couple of months, but he knew he wanted to marry her. They planned to live in Los Angeles and have children.

I think that all of the stories in this book are miracles, but this one is a double miracle.

From Mental Illness To The Stage

I've heard people say you have to be crazy to be a comedian and get on stage trying to make strangers laugh. Take it from me, it's one of the hardest things you can do.

People say that public speaking is everyone's greatest fear. Multiply that by 100 if you want to try stand-up comedy. Maria Bamford who I have met several times grew up not knowing she had Obsessive Compulsive Disorder, more commonly referred to as OCD.

She had no idea she would later go on to be diagnosed as bipolar as well. The daughter of a Dad who was a dermatologist, and a Mom who was a therapist didn't help, and they put her into therapy when she was 10. She says she would weep uncontrollably if someone looked at her wrong.

At 21 she entered a program for an eating disorder and was put on anti-depressants. She had always wanted to be a comedian but was led to believe it wasn't a particularly viable career choice for a girl.

She graduated college with a degree in English literature and wound up waiting tables for a while but at 25 decided to move out to L.A. to try her hand at comedy, where she worked hard and made a name for herself.

By the age of 40 she had released three comedy albums, starred in a film with Zach Galifianakis, and was touring the world, but that year she became suicidal and had a total meltdown.

That's when she was diagnosed as being bipolar. She was in and out of psych wards from 2010 to 2012 and was put on heavy meds.

In 2013 while rebuilding her life she met the creator of Arrested Development who cast her in the Netflix reboot of the series. He also helped her develop the concept for her Netflix TV show *Lady Dynamite* in which she basically played herself as a comedian working to rebuild her life after a mental breakdown.

In person she is charming. I last saw her at the Just for Laughs Festival in Montreal, which is the biggest comedy festival in the world, and where I do interviews every year on the red carpet for the Just for Laughs Awards.

She is sweet, funny and approachable, and very open to discussing what she's been through. It's very endearing. She's still performing actively, has been in many TV shows and films, often as Executive Producer, and is loved by everyone in comedy.

Judd Apatow is quoted as saying she's the funniest woman in the world.

She met her husband Scott on the dating site Ok Cupid, and they married in 2015. In the People Magazine article about her in 2016 she said "He was so accepting of my mental health history. Being in a psych ward made me realize that you can't wait to be a perfect person to commit to a relationship."

The Book That Changed His Life

I absolutely LOVE this story. In 2005 Canadian born William Paul Young was working three jobs trying to keep afloat, in order to take care of his wife and four of his six children who all lived in a small 900 square foot apartment.

He had lost his home to bankruptcy in 2004 due to some bad investments and even worse choices, and his wife Kim had been after him to write something about his relationship with G-d to give to their children as a gift.

With Christmas coming and no money for presents he began working on what he thought would be something for his children and maybe some family members. Previously he had only written some short stories and poetry.

As a bit of back story, his parents were Christian evangelicals who moved to New Guinea when he was only one year old to work with a stone-age tribe called the Dani tribe, some of whom still practiced cannibalism.

They were the only white people the tribe had ever seen, and he was basically raised with them, and learned to speak their language. Some of the members of the tribe began sexually abusing him, which happened to him again by some older boys when his parents sent him to a boarding school on the coast of West Papua a year later.

The family returned to Canada when he was 10, and because his father became an itinerant pastor never living too long in one place, he went to 13 different schools before he graduated from high school.

He wound up in Oregon where he met his wife Kim, and started raising his family, but never dealt with the wounds from his past. In my book *Healing Your Heart, by Changing Your Mind* I explain how these traumatic "heart wounds" stay with you your entire life and affect everything you do, until you learn to release yourself from the power they hold over you.

In 1994 his wife found out he had been having a three-month affair with her best friend and in coming clean he disclosed the stories from his past. It took them many years for them to work through that, but they managed to stay together.

For the next 11 years he worked on himself to unravel all the pain he was holding inside. Fast forward to 2005 he had a 40-minute daily train commute to work, and that's when he began taking notes to write the novel his wife had been asking him to write.

Again, he thought it would be read by his family and maybe a few friends. He was off by more than 20 million people.

The book was called *The Shack.* It was about a father whose mourning of the death of his daughter brings a visit from G-d, and it has become one of the best-selling books of all time and made him a millionaire.

The article in the New York Post on December 16, 2016 was because the book had also been made into a film that would be opening in a few months, with G-d being played by an African-American woman, Octavia Spencer.

The fascinating part was how the book even came to be, because of all the obstacles facing its production. It took William about six months to write, and then he got 26 rejections from every publishing house he submitted it to. Boy I bet they were sorry!

He scraped together enough money to have 15 copies made at Office Depot and gave them to his children and a few friends. But the friends shared it with other friends, and all of a sudden, he was getting a lot of demand for more books and for discussions about the book.

He reached out to an author he barely knew for advice, and that author sent it to a friend who thought it would make a great film. They made a plan to try and sell 100,000 copies over five years to help finance the movie, not knowing that most best sellers only need to sell 7500 copies to achieve that status.

After getting the 26 rejections they decided to open their own publishing business, spent $300. on a website and some promotion, and ordered 10,000 copies selling them out of the house.

They had 1,000 pre-orders before the book was even printed and between May of 2007 and June of 2008, they had sold 1.1 million copies. That allowed William Young to quit his jobs, just to have the time to deal with all the opportunities that came his way.

Hachette handled world-wide sales and Barnes and Noble placed it at the front of all their stores. It was printed in 48 languages and in June of 2008 it hit No. 1 on the New York Times best-seller list and stayed there for 49 weeks.

At the time of the writing of the article it had been on the list for 136 weeks and was then No. 7. Needless to say, he bought a big house for his family and went on to write two more religious themed novels, all of which did well.

But he says the real gift out of all of it was not so much the money, but his Spiritual growth and maturity that led to his success. He was quoted as saying, 'When you live without expectations, everything becomes a gift. In that I'm a very blessed man."

<u>Burned Beyond Recognition</u>

Burns are one of the most horrible injuries that anyone can endure. Anyone who has ever burnt themselves on anything can attest to that.

Even a second-degree sunburn can be unbearable, but having third degree burns on more than 60% of your body is unfathomable.

I've met some of our brave wounded warriors, injured in combat, who survived disfiguring facial burns in the war and have overcome their self-consciousness who now make appearances all over as motivational speakers, and some even do comedy.

Like my friend Bobby Henline, who was wounded in Iraq in 2007 and burned over nearly 50% of his body including severe burns to his face.

After a very long recuperation period and many surgeries in which he had to lose parts of his ears, and his left arm below his elbow, he has turned to stand-up comedy to ease the pain, and at the time of the NPR story about him he was performing regularly at the Rivercenter Comedy Club in San Antonio, Texas, where he lived with his wife Connie.

I have actually been in that comedy club, and know the owner, and wound up meeting Bobby some years later at a comedy show in New York. I was so impressed with him as a comedian and as a person. He opens by making jokes about his appearance, which is basically taking back the power by saying things about yourself before other people do.

Self-deprecating humor can be very powerful, but you have to be secure enough with yourself in order to be able to do it!

But my story here is about another person. A woman named Turia Pitt.

In 2011, Turia Pitt was a gorgeous model in Australia in the middle of running a 62-mile ultra-marathon, … which I didn't even know was a thing, … through the Australian Outback, when she was engulfed in flames by a freak firestorm that chased her down.

Before she knew it her arms and legs were on fire and her face literally melted. If you saw photos of her before you'd see that she possessed the type of beauty that few were ever graced with.

Everyone wants to look their best and for many women, … and men too, … their looks mean everything to them. Turia made a living off of her looks.

How she even survived was a miracle because doctors gave her a very small chance of making it through. It took four hours for help to reach her as she waited on a hill in indescribable pain, in the hot Australian sun with five other injured runners.

She lost seven of her fingers, spent over six months in the hospital, endured over 200 operations, and more than two years in recovery.

There were not enough skin grafts available in Australia for her because she had been burned so severely, and her surgeons had to beg Customs to let them import skin from the United States, which at the time was not allowed in Australia.

They collected forty-eight skin grafts, primarily from the backs, legs, buttocks, and abdomens of recently deceased people to use in the multiple operations that gave her back a face and covered her badly burnt body.

Through her entire ordeal and recovery, which included the aforementioned 200 plus surgeries, her high school boyfriend Michael Hoskin was by her side encouraging her with the thought that she could make it.

The article I read about her in 2016 in the New York Post was because she had just done the unthinkable and ran her first Ironman competition, and followed that up by running the Ironman World Championship in Kona, Hawaii.

She was quoted as saying, "Kona was a grueling experience that taught me over and over again that when we get our mindset right, we can truly achieve anything.

She has gone on to become a best-selling author, a motivational speaker as so many people do who rise above their devastating obstacles, and she works with Interplast, a charity that provides free reconstructive surgery to people in poor countries who couldn't otherwise afford it.

As an update, during her time in intensive care Michael bought her an engagement ring, and since this story aired in 2016, they married and had a child. This man is an angel and when he looks into her eyes, which she was able to save by closing them while she was on fire, he says he still sees her inner beauty. What a great man!

CHAPTER 11

From The Year 2017

From Paralyzed To Paris, ... No Bull

Bonner Bolton started riding bulls at the age of 10. His father Toya Bolton was a famous rodeo cowboy who moved the family to Paris to be in Buffalo Bill's Wild West Show at Euro Disney.

After a year they returned to their ranch in Texas. Bonner grew up riding horses and working with cattle. It's all he knew and all he wanted to do.

In 2017 when the article in the New York Post was written there was to be a Professional Bull Riders event at Madison Square Garden but Bonner who had finished 4th overall in the world championship bull riding competition in Las Vegas had an accident that would change his life forever.

He was riding a huge bull named Cowboy Up and when he went to dismount, the bull bucked, and he was thrown off and landed on his head. He heard the crack and knew what had happened.

He couldn't feel his arms or his legs. He was paralyzed.

After being rushed to the hospital, the doctors said he had broken his C2 vertebra which is what happened to Christopher (Superman) Reeve, and what landed him in a wheelchair for the rest of his life.

Bonner was totally paralyzed for 24 hours when an absolute miracle occurred, and he felt the feeling come back into his body. The doctors were amazed and said that maybe only 2% of people would walk away from that severe of a spinal injury.

He endured a six-hour operation in which they implanted a steel rod in his neck to stabilize him plus a metal frame around his neck to hold things in place.

His recovery was slow and painful, and he used cryotherapy combined with his hot tub, low-impact movements in the water of his pool, tai chi in steam rooms, and hot yoga classes in order to help him heal.

After a few months his sports doctor told him he'd never be able to ride again due to the placement of the metal in his neck, because if he had another accident, he'd either be totally paralyzed or die.

But in 2015 at the world championship, he was there as an observer, when he caught the eye of IMG Models honcho Ivan Bart who offered to sign the handsome young man to a modeling contract. He said the modeling contract gave him a fresh start on a new life.

In a year's time he wound up in Paris where he met with fashion photographers, and at the big Madison Square Garden event he didn't wind up riding, but he wound up hosting fashion editors in his role as the sport's ambassador, since WME-IMG bought the Professional Bull Riders in April of 2015.

Since then, he's posed for several fashion campaigns and hopes to pursue an acting career. Talking about the accident he said, "There's no explanation other than it wasn't meant for my life to end that day, and for me to become permanently paralyzed. There was something more for me to do."

The next year after the article in 2017 he appeared on Dancing With The Stars, dancing with Sharna Burgess who seems to get dance partners who have had a bit of trauma in their lives, and he was featured on Entertainment Tonight.

Disabled Actors In Off-Broadway Play

In 2017 an article came out in the New York Post stating that 19% of Americans have some form of a disability. For that reason, several off-Broadway plays have been hiring actors and performers with true disabilities.

And often they're in wheelchairs on stage when they don't use them in real life.

Such was the case with a play called *Cost of Living* that featured two actors that fell into that category. Gregg Mozgala was born with Cerebral Palsy, and Katy Sullivan was born without lower legs.

When they came out for their curtain call the audience was shocked. They had no idea.

The playwright purposely chose actors with disabilities rather than choose an actor who could pretend to limp.

In a revival of Tennessee Williams' *The Glass Menagerie* one of the leads, Madison Ferris is a beautiful young woman with Muscular Dystrophy, who performed her part in a wheelchair.

At the time of the writing of the article, an actor named Evan Ruggiero, who lost a leg to cancer, was killing it in an off–Broadway play called *Bastard Jones*, and the director was quoted as saying that he even questions the word "disability."

He went on to say that "Evan has abilities many people don't, … for instance I can't tap dance on one leg!"

The actors themselves said they prefer the word "disabled" rather than the P.C. term "differently abled." When that comes up in the play "Cost of Living" Gregg Mozgala's character says, "Stop it, that's f^@king retarded!" And the line gets a big laugh!

CHAPTER 12

From The Year 2018

One Armed MMA Fighter

Being an MMA fighter takes tremendous skill and a lot of courage. That is exemplified by Nick Newell, who was born with his left arm ending just below the elbow.

Six years before, back in 2012, Ultimate Fighting Championship head Dana White had turned Nick down to be one of his fighters, thinking it would be too dangerous for him to fight.

But in 2018 he had to give in. He was quoted as saying to Nick at a press conference, "This is crazy man, but I'm going to do it. I'm going to give you your chance."

Nick was quoted as saying, "At the end of the day I'm not a one-handed MMA fighter. I'm an MMA fighter who just happens to have one hand. Even after I was already established people would tell me what I can and can't accomplish. I have a strong belief in myself."

Why do people do that? Why do people try and limit other people's dreams? What do they possibly get out of it?

Maybe in some way it makes them not regret the things in life that THEY didn't go for themselves, because if a one-armed man could become an MMA fighter what might THEY have been able to accomplish having all of their limbs?

Nick first tried wrestling in high school in Milford, CT where he's from, but he didn't like it and was ready to quit until his parents talked him into sticking with it. Now he says he's grateful for that input.

He started winning matches and ended up the two-time captain of the wrestling team at Western New England University in Springfield, Mass. where he went to school and became interested in MMA.

He got a job in post-production at The History Channel and started training for MMA. He won his first professional fight in 2014, and as his popularity grew, parents of children with similar challenges reached out to him for advice, making him realize how many people were in the same situation.

He said he was inspired by a couple of other athletes who only had one arm like Shaquem Griffin, a one-handed linebacker on the Seattle Seahawks, and one-handed MLB pitcher Jim Abbott, who as many people with disabilities do became a motivational speaker after he retired from baseball.

These are stories that people need to hear to inspire them to live their dreams. In any case he was signed to appear on Dana White's Tuesday Night Contender Series on July 24, 2018, and he lost that bout.

But he went on to attain a professional record of 16 wins and only 3 losses. In July of 2010 he signed a deal with Bellator MMA who he is still signed to after winning his first fight in the first round.

He's married and had a baby boy named Wyatt in 2018, and he is just another great example that nothing can stop certain people if their will to succeed is strong enough.

CHAPTER 13

From The Year 2019

Five Hundred Fifty Pound Marathon Runner?

I have no idea how some people can run marathons, ... 26 miles. It amazes me yet many people do it. Even 3 miles sounds like an awful lot to me, especially when it's an obstacle course, where you have to climb over walls, swim beneath underwater barriers, and swing from ropes.

Jose Cordero did it as part of the Spartan Race series after an 11-year transformation when he went from 550 pounds all the way down to 220 pounds.

In his 2019 article in the New York Post, he was quoted as saying "It showed me that I could do a lot of things I didn't think I could do."

Growing up in Elizabeth, New Jersey to an Italian mother and a Hispanic father he said the house was always packed with food and all they did was "eat, eat, eat."

By his mid 30's he was up to 550 pounds, and he couldn't sit behind counters or fit into certain cars. In 2008 he went for gastric bypass surgery where they told him he'd likely only lose 100 pounds, but he did it anyway, despite tremendous fear of the safety of the procedure.

In the first month afterwards, he could only eat liquids like broth and Crystal Light. He started walking and lifting light weights before his doctors even gave him permission. Initially he could only walk a mile.

Soon he was up to four miles. All he did was work at his own IT company, and then exercise in his home gym. After five months he was down 100 pounds, after working out every day and eating only yogurt, baby food, rice and veggies.

Two years later, in 2010 he hit his goal of 170 pounds. His whole life changed, and he actually became a ski instructor. At the time of the writing of the article he had also ended a 3 ½ year relationship he had been in.

He started working out at the gym instead of only at home because he was no longer ashamed for people to see his body. He says that keeping the weight off is an ongoing challenge.

He works out for 90 minutes six or seven days a week, doing both cardio and strength training, and watches what he eats. He never eats after 7 P.M. That takes real discipline. Some people advise not eating after 10 P.M. but 7 P.M. is very admirable.

In 2017 he worked with a trainer who competed in Spartan Races and got him interested in doing the same. He took Life Time Fitness classes to prepare and he said that setting goals like having the date of an obstacle race has been very influential in the success he has achieved.

Since that first race in May of 2019, he signed up for two more, and then signed up for seven in 2020, including one that's 13 miles long and known as "the Beast." He's since been featured on The Today Show telling his inspirational story.

Being that I'm writing this book in the midst of the pandemic I don't know if he was able to participate in any races this year, since some of them have had to be rescheduled, but he says he likes the Spartan World because after so many years of being isolated when he was so heavy, he loves the camaraderie. He said, "You're gaining community. It's indescribable."

Jeffrey@JeffreyGurian.com

CHAPTER 14

From The Year 2020

Superhero With Genetic Disease

HBO Max has a superhero series called *Doom Patrol* which features a very unique cast of superheroes, not with your usual run-of-the-mill superpowers.

Character Dorothy Spinner who is the product of a mating between a man and a "primitive woman" he met in 1917 has the ability to manifest anything she imagines.

She also has a deformed face that they describe as resembling an ape, and a group of imaginary friends that she can't seem to control.

She's played by a 20-year-old actress named Abigail Shapiro, who has a genetic disease called Cleidocranial Dysplasia, which is a birth defect that affects the bones and teeth. For some reason it often affects the collar bones which can be completely absent allowing the person who has it to touch their shoulders together.

It's what Gaten Matarazzo has who plays Dustin on the Netflix series *Stranger Things*.

In Abigail Shapiro's case she shares the condition with both her mother and sister but received treatment for it at a very young age. For being chosen to play this role she received an article in the NY Post.

She was a student at Fordham University when she received the news that she was cast in the part. When she was just 12, she played the part of Cindy Lou in *How the Grinch Stole Christmas! The Musical,* at Madison Square Garden, and at 13 she and her sister Milly performed their own original cabaret show at the prestigious venue Feinstein's 54 Below in Manhattan.

She's also an accomplished opera singer and the sister of political commentator Ben Shapiro, as well as an activist working hard to bring attention to those suffering with CCD.

Out Of Sight

I think it's very fitting to end this book with a story that we're all aware of. On May 8th of 2020 the New York Post did a story honoring the 70th birthday of music legend Stevie Wonder who went blind as an infant, but had an incredible music career, ... and still has one, ... that influenced generations of musicians that followed.

In 2005 in an article in People Magazine he was quoted as saying "I want my music to encourage people to understand that what the world needs is positivity, and that isn't something that happens by happenstance. It is something that you have to commit yourself to every day by the way you treat your fellow man."

That is the essence of why I wrote this book. My personal goal in everything I do has always been to put positive energy out to The Universe, which I was able to do as a Cosmetic Dentist, as a clinical professor, as a stuttering therapist, and in my comedy career.

Little Stevie Wonder as he was known in the beginning, made his debut at the legendary Apollo Theatre in Harlem in 1962, at only 12 years old. He was so nervous that he dropped his bongos, but only ten years later won his first three Grammys.

Stevie Wonder has amassed 25 Grammy Awards, including the most prestigious of them all The Album of the Year award, which he won three times, a record only matched by Frank Sinatra and Paul Simon.

Some of his other highlights were in 1980 he was influential in establishing Martin Luther King's birthday as a national holiday, and added his *Happy Birthday* track as it's musical anthem. Then in 1982 he did a duet with Paul McCartney on the song *Ebony and Ivory*, which is why some people say he is "The Beatles of Black music."

Then in 1999 he did the Super Bowl halftime show with Gloria Estefan, and in 2012 he did a Royal Performance for Queen Elizabeth along with Paul McCartney, Elton John and Ed Sheeran.

I think his example of positivity and inspiration is the perfect story on which to end this book.

Of course there are endless examples of other stories across the world of people who have overcome what appeared to be seemingly impossible obstacles, to achieve their goals. But I limited this book to the stories that crossed my own personal path over the last 21 years, where I was inspired to stop what I was doing for a minute, and go get a pair of scissors to cut them out, in order to save them in a folder so that some day in the future I could present them to YOU!

Some years back I attended a session of the National Speakers Association in San Francisco, and was privileged to hear several motivational speakers who rose above what some people might consider to be limitations, like a Wounded Warrior with a severely scarred face as the result of burns, or like John Foppe, another man born without arms whose parents refused to help him put on his pants until he figured out how to do it on his own.

He learned to use his feet the way other people use their hands. Now he travels the world as a motivational speaker and author, with a wife and family.

And also take notice how many of these people went on to find mates, get married and have children when the singles bars are filled with people without so-called disabilities!

I also admire groups like The Mouth and Foot Painting Artists who I contribute to every year for the greeting cards and calendars they send me, done by artists with no arms who literally paint and draw with their mouths and feet.

These are the people who inspire me to do better, when I think I can't.

I hope that some of you will use this book to create your own story of overcoming an obstacle, giving you the Happiness and freedom you not only deserve, but were born to have!

As my friend, the late, great Dr. Wayne Dyer used to wish me, "I send you Love and all green lights."

EPILOGUE

I truly hope that this book has been as helpful to you as it was to me while writing it. Researching and writing about these courageous people has given me a source of strength and the knowledge to hope I can handle whatever comes my way.

Life tends to throw unexpected obstacles in our path and how we handle them often determines the course of the rest of our lives. Engaging in self-pity is one of the worst things we can do for ourselves.

I stopped collecting these inspirational stories in 2020 but as I was writing this epilogue in 2021, I came across one more story that I felt I had to include about a blind actor named Adam Morse.

The story appeared in the NY Post and was about Adam not only acting but doing his own stunts on the action-heavy Apple TV Plus series called "See" without the use of either a cane or a guide dog.

He's 31 years old and says he spent a few days training with a fight choreographer, who offered to have a "stunt double" do the fight scenes but Adam was adamant in doing them himself. I wonder if that's where the word "adamant" comes from! (LOL)

After a full day of sword fighting, people on the set reluctantly approached him and asked if he was truly sightless or not. He said he thrives on "exceeding expectations."

Adam joined the series on August 27, 2021, which is set in what the NY Post describes as a "dystopian-yet-primitive future where most of humanity is sightless due to a virus." Sighted people are branded heretics!

Jason Momoa from Game of Thrones is one of the stars. Adam is also a director, writer and producer, and had already been working in Hollywood at the time he lost his sight back in 2009 due to a rare mitochondrial disease.

He claims, "Losing my eyesight was the start of my Spiritual journey, and I had to accept it wasn't a curse and that it was my choice on how it would determine my future."

He was also quoted as saying "I've been actively reprogramming myself every day mentally to be positive and strong and to think about how my condition can elevate me as an artist, so that I can find the blessing in this situation, and appreciate that I was being put on a new path."

This is exactly the kind of Spiritual message I like to write about. He says when he was first diagnosed, he went through a very dark and pessimistic period where he basically gave up on his dreams. In addition to sword fighting on the show he also rides horses and credits his sense of confidence in himself to his ability to do all these things.

He learns his lines by using a script reading software, and sometimes has to "feel out" his marks so he knows where to physically stand during a scene, but he makes it work due to his determination.

His goal is to become the first blind action hero, taking roles that no one would expect him to be able to play, whether he's behind the wheel of a car in a chase scene, or running around a battlefield.

These are the kind of stories I hope you will remember when facing obstacles of your own. I hope you never have to face any obstacles at all, but if you do I hope these stories will stay with you and give you hope.

Thank you so much for reading my book. **Please read below for your free offer!!!**

To sign up for my mailing list and receive a free gift, and a complimentary 15 minute private Skype call with me, please use the landing page on my website at https://mailchi.mp/jeffreygurian/healingyourheart

If you liked this book, you will probably also like the other two books in what I refer to as my "Happiness Series."

Healing Your Heart by Changing Your Mind— *A Spiritual and Humorous Approach To Achieving Happiness* is available as an e-book, a paperback and an audio book, has 255 mostly 5-star reviews as of this writing, and can be found on Amazon at this link: **https://www.amazon.com/dp/0692982515**

Fight The Fear—*Overcoming Obstacles That Stand In Your Way* is available as an e-book and a paperback and currently has 79 all five-star reviews and the link on Amazon is: **https://www.amazon.com/dp/1735442607**

If you have any questions or positive comments, I can be reached at **jeffrey@jeffreygurian.com**

If you know anyone who stutters please ask them to look at my website:
https://www.stopstutteringnowgurian.com

On Instagram I am **@jeffreygurian**

To support the work:
https://www.patreon.com/comedymatterstv

As a help to future readers, if you enjoyed this book, it would be really helpful if you'd be kind enough to leave a positive review on the Amazon page, which is how Amazon ranks it's books, ... and maybe tell a couple of friends about it!

Thank you again so very much for taking the time to read my book!

THE END

Made in the USA
Middletown, DE
04 August 2024